A scholarly and exciting study of the post-conquest condition of the Walapai and Havasupai Indians of the 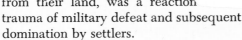 Canyon region in the late nin century. The millennial Ghost movement, which believers felt magically cause all Whites to be from their land, was a reaction trauma of military defeat and subsequent domination by settlers.

As the noted anthropologist, Edward H. Spicer, has written in his foreword, "The authors refrain from unwarranted generalization, but they have collected an abundance of data which enable us to relate what happened among the Pai to what has happened in many other parts of the world as people have sought to find ways out of oppressive conditions threatening their very identity. The authors are to be commended on a significant piece of work in the best anthropological tradition."

the southwestern United States. He has published scientific monographs and numerous papers in both English and Spanish.

Robert C. Euler

Dr. Robert C. Euler is Chairman of the Center for Anthropological Studies at Prescott College. Formerly Chairman of the Department of Anthropology at the University of Utah, he has conducted research and published scientific papers in archaeology, ethnology, ethnohistory and culture change of Southwestern and Great Basin American Indians. He serves as anthropological consultant to the Hualapai Tribe.

The Ghost Dance of 1889

The Ghost Dance of 1889

AMONG THE PAI INDIANS OF NORTHWESTERN ARIZONA

By

Henry F. Dobyns *and* Robert C. Euler

PRESCOTT COLLEGE PRESS · 1967

Prescott College Studies In Anthropology No. 1

Foreword

THIS STUDY OF THE GHOST DANCE among the Pai is a notable contribution to our understanding of cultural history in the Southwest. There should be no compartmentalization between historical research with documents and ethnographic field research with living informants. The present study brings together, with great success, results from earlier and recent field studies and the contemporary documentation. The product is a vivid picture of the situation of the Walapai and Havasupai Indians in the 1880's and 1890's when the fever of the Ghost Dance arose among them. The religious activity of the Indians was a reaction against the desperate conditions in which the Whites in northwestern Arizona had placed them. The nature of the White aggression is detailed in concrete fashion and thus illuminates the rationale of the Ghost Dance. We see how this was a part of what was happening all through the West at this time as White aggression began to overwhelm the small tribes of the region. The authors illustrate the valued blend of the historical and the ethnographic approaches.

The study does not stop with description, but proceeds to present the Pai Ghost Dance as an instance of a more general phenomenon. In so doing it contributes to that general knowledge which anthropology seeks to develop in its comparative study of all human situations. It makes clear that the Ghost Dance was not only an interesting series of events in Southwestern history. It is also an example of a recurrent phenomenon in human history, that of the millennial movement, which has frequently followed in the wake of conquest and oppression. The authors refrain from unwarranted generalization, but they have collected an abundance of data which enable us to relate what happened among the Pai to what has happened in many other parts of the world as people have sought to find ways out of oppressive conditions threatening their very identity. The authors are to be commended on a significant piece of work in the best anthropological tradition.

Edward H. Spicer
The University of Arizona

Preface

A CENTURY AGO, the Pai Indians were a tribe of fierce mountain warriors, known as the Walapai and Havasupai to a handful of Arizona pioneers and to U.S. troops who campaigned against them starting in 1866. In three years, the Pai were defeated and forced to abandon their aboriginal life and to yield their lands to settlers, miners and ranchers. So severe was their cultural shock at Anglo-American impact, that only recently have the Pai begun to achieve security as an ethnic group.

One of the major Pai responses to this trauma was religious in nature and, though short lived, this response subsequently had far-reaching effects on Pai religious beliefs and practices.

The northeastern Pai Indians surviving today in northwest central Arizona worship in a variety of ways. Some attend services at a Christian mission in the depths of Cataract Canyon; others go to a Latter-day Saints chapel or to an evangelical church in Peach Springs; some are Presbyterians; still others carry on an attenuated form of native Pai religion; and a few participate in no organized form of religion at all.

This diversity of religious belief among a group of only a few hundred Indians represents one consequence of their forceful incorporation into the general population of the United States. It came about relatively recently as part of a general trend toward religious diversification among tribes of the American Southwest resulting from proselytization by Christian priests and missionaries (Spicer 1962: 502-38). Until 1889, all Pai shared a common tribal religion that probably had changed little for many centuries (Dobyns and Euler 1960: 49-57). While some Pai individuals ceased to believe very fervently in the tribal religion 20 years prior to 1889, only in that year did a major innovation appear in Pai religious practices and beliefs. In 1889, northeastern Pai religious unity was broken for the first time by the conversion of many of the Pai to a new faith that swept through numerous tribes in the western United States. This messianic movement quickly became known as the "ghost dance" because of the Indians' belief that proper dancing would magically restore deceased Indians and game animals to life while doing away with the conquering white man and his oppressions.

This millenial religion was, like others of its type, concerned with the redistribution of power. Its adherents, forcibly joined to the dominant Anglo-American society, constituted that social segment with the least power in its own homeland. The ghost dance movement offered the Pai a "fantasy compensation for practical disappointments," and a substitute for political action (Mair 1959: 119). The traditional Pai religion proved incapable of giving Pai believers all they expected from it under post-contact conditions. Although the ghost dance contained numerous formal similarities to traditional Pai rituals, its core doctrine, involving resurrection and a messiah-like figure similar to Christianity's Jesus, differed from the Pai aboriginal religion.

Once broken, Pai religious unity was never restored after the initial diversification fostered by the ghost dance cult. Anglo-American missionaries, arriving on the heels of the decline in nativistic fervor, began converting demoralized Pai to evangelical forms of Christianity. They found their task easier because of the ghost dance. Thus, the foundation of contemporary diversity in Pai religious worship can be located in the disruptive influence of the ghost dance.

The year 1889 stands out in northeastern Pai religious history as the divide between native tribal worship and modern diversity of belief.

In this study, the authors attempt to examine in some detail the ghost dance movement and the beginnings of religious diversity among the northeastern Pai in 1889 and immediately subsequent years.

In addition, the study undertakes an exercise in ethnohistorical methodology combining (1) ethnological analyses of Indian statements obtained in 1918 and 1929, (2) interviewers' transcriptions of these data, (3) Indian statements obtained by us during the years 1952-57, and (4) newspaper reports contemporary with the events. This methodological exercise has been undertaken in part because of apparent confusion among anthropologists concerning the relative reliability of various types of sources of information about human culture. This problem can be exemplified in writings by an eminent anthropologist, George P. Murdock. In one place, he claims that he "can see no sound reason for differentially estimating the reliability of findings" obtained by "observations made in on-going cultures," and by "questioning of older informants about the way of life which prevailed before" provided that "sound field methods have been employed in both types of situation" (Murdock 1963: 541). Elsewhere, he takes the position that informant testimony is quite unreliable (Murdock 1959: 43).

While occasionally one finds a reliable respondent with excellent recall (Euler 1966a), in general we note a difference between statements by participants in events and the oral traditions of the events obtained later in time from non-participants. We regard this as a difference too great to be overcome by sound field methods. The high proportion of the analysis to follow which has been taken from newspaper files illustrates this point.

In addition, the data employed produce a fuller, more detailed and more accurate record of the ghost dance movement among the Pai than has heretofore been published. This makes available for increasingly accurate comparative analysis of messianic movements (which we hope will build on existing comparative formulations) detailed eyewitness accounts previously hidden in the relatively inaccessible files of an obscure rural newspaper. In publishing this analysis, we are also complying with the scientific obligation to make available a revised version of one of the manuscripts on which part of the analysis of messianic movements and northeastern Pai history contained in *Cycles of Conquest* (Spicer 1962: 272-3, 594) rests.

Henry F. Dobyns
University of Kentucky

Robert C. Euler
Prescott College

Table of Contents

ILLUSTRATIONS

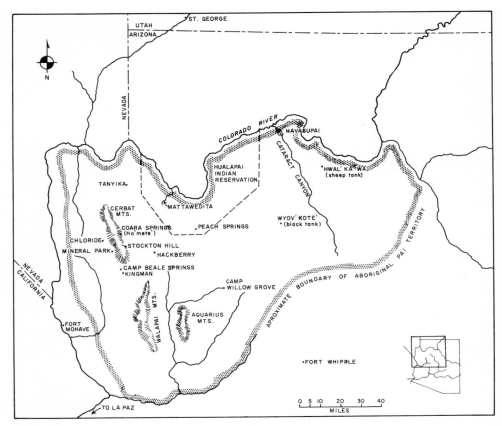

Aboriginal Pai Territory

THE GHOST DANCE MOVEMENT

THE GHOST DANCE MOVEMENT swept through the northeastern Pai more than a generation after the beginning of white settlement in their territory and almost two generations after the first Pai contacts with Anglo-Americans.

The ghost dance, for a time, became fairly widespread in the western United States. The Pai borrowed it from their Southern Paiute neighbors to the north who had been subjected to much the same stresses of conquest as had the Pai (Euler 1966b). The Southern Paiute, in turn, had been converted to the movement by the Northern Paiute who generated the cult during the later years of the 19th Century. The movement diffused to Indians in the western states "in two distinct waves, one about 1870, the second about 1890." The central doctrine of both these movements was that dead Indians would return to life and prosperous aboriginal conditions would be restored if the ghost dance rituals were properly performed. Little is known of the diffusion of the 1870 movement except that it moved "largely westward into southeastern Oregon and California, that it survived but four or five years at most . . ." (Gayton 1930:57-8), with important effects on Northwest Coast Indians (Nash 1955: 412ff).

So far as present knowledge goes, there is no record of the 1870 ghost dance movement having spread to the Pai. The series of religious variations that began among the Pai in 1889, however, is fairly well documented, and demonstrated the deep emotional and psychological attachment of these Indians to their ancestral lands and traditional way of life, both visibly lost for the most part to Anglo-American encroachment in the decades just preceding. Only under conditions of severe stress were the Pai able to accept an outside religious movement, the ghost dance, with its associated creed centering on magical restoration of former lands and customs, and perform rituals dictated by that alien ideology.

[1]

The ghost dance among the Pai was a response to a group trauma resulting from the Pai's demoralizing contact with Anglo-Americans. The overall ghost dance movement has, indeed, been called one "phase of a recurrent series of messianic or revivalistic movements which have arisen among the weaker peoples throughout the world as reactionary waves to the crushing impact of European culture" (DuBois 1939: v). Among the Pai, the ghost dance was a specific response to Anglo-American domination with all that this meant in loss of land and resources, in forced adjustments to and changes in social activities, beliefs, habits and even actual subsistence. Had the Pai not had an emotionally and psychologically deep attachment to and dependence on their lands, the trauma of Anglo-American impact might not have been so sharp.

By borrowing a neighboring tribe's religious nativism in the ghost dance rather than inventing a form of nativism within the traditional Pai ritual, the Pai opened the way for later and greater diversification in religious practice and belief which produced permanent changes in this whole sphere of northeastern Pai culture.

Ghost Dance Form

The ghost dance among the Pai followed a pattern of dancing already familiar to them. Scudder Mekeel's brief summary (Kroeber 1935: 198) was reconstructed from informant descriptions. "The dance was by men and women placed alternately in a circle revolving slowly about a pole which was spirally painted and had eagle feathers at the top . . . Feathers were worn on the head; there seems to have been no standardized or prescribed costume." That statement is at variance with 1929 informant descriptions, with 1952-7 informant recall, and with the 1890 published accounts that prescribed well-cleansed white clothing for the dancers. "The clothing they wore was all white" (authors' field notes). Old Mike's 1929 description of a dance held at Grass Springs (Tanyika) was more detailed:

"When night came all the girls and boys (younger women and men) started to dance in a ring, alternating and holding hands. They started circling with a short step when the singing began. They alternated in clockwise and counterclockwise direction. In

[2]

Typical Pai camp scene during the Ghost Dance years. Photo by George Wharton James, courtesy Southwest Museum.

the center there was a fire, and there were also fires on the outside at some distance. The older people of my age stayed by the fire and watched the young people dance. Jeff knew the Paiute song and he sang.

"The boys wore their underwear and the girls wore white cloth dresses like coveralls. They painted their faces with qwada (red hematite) and matinyatc.

"They stopped dancing at midnight. Jeff spoke to them, 'After this we are going to have another dance in six days' " (Kroeber 1935: 200).

A contemporary newspaper account also noted the white costume: "The dance is kept up continually for several days and is followed by a feast. The dancers are dressed in white . . ." (MCM Nov. 29, 1890).

Our western Pai informants remembered additional aspects of formal patterning of the ghost dance besides the wearing of white: "They danced in a circle to the left. They alternated a man and a woman. There can't be two women — they have a rule against that. They have guards to watch called 'alalga. They replaced a man or woman as necessary. The Indians put a long pole in the center of the the circle and on top of it were tied an eagle's feathers. They had no music or drum — just singing" (authors' field notes). Our informants of the 1952-7 period appear, however, to have forgotten that rattles actually were used to accompany the dance. "There was singing at the Ghost Dance and gourds were carried by both sexes" (Kroeber 1935: 201).

In the beginning of ghost dancing, "Jeff brought in the Paiute song. Two or three years later he introduced his own song dreamed from God. After that both Paiute and Jeff's songs were used" (Kroeber 1935: 201). One of our informants claimed that the Paiute also introduced rasping sticks to the Pai to accompany the ghost dance songs (see below).

Anglo-Americans visiting Grass Springs in order to find out what the Indians actually were engaged in, furnished the *Mohave County Miner* staff more eyewitness description of the ghost dance in 1889 which confirms the white costume, describes a brush windbreak built around the dance ground, and dates the introduction of this messianic ritual among the Pai.

"There are about five hundred Walapais attending the dance. They have built a brush fence about five feet high and enclosing a square of about 150 feet of ground, which is cleared and leveled and in which they dance. All the Indians that can get in this space engage in dancing. The dance commences at sundown and lasts until sunrise, when all the dancers go to the spring and bathe. The dancers are dressed in white. This dance is a new one for the Wallapais and the ceremony was introduced by the medicine men for the first time this year. The medicine men claim that if the dance is kept up long enough that those who participate in it will be able to see and talk with departed relatives and friends . . ." (MCM Sept. 28, 1889).

Another eyewitness description of a ghost dance held in the Cerbat Mountains some 30 miles north of Kingman in 1891 was published.

"As darkness began to fall, the every-day flashy, though scant clothing was exchanged for the white robes prescribed by the medicine men as a dancing costume; faces and hair were painted white, forming the most ghastly picture conceivable. A favorite mode of painting seemed to be to paint the lips, eyes, nose and hair white, leaving the rest of the face its natural color . . . [Dancers are said to have painted their faces white with 'emete, red with ookwata and black with 'oomwhaja (authors' field notes).]

"Imagine a circular piece of ground one hundred feet in diameter, enclosed by a fence, made by putting poles and bushes into the ground, and surrounded by high and rugged granite walls that reflect in demoniacal fantasies the lurid lights of a half dozen fires that blaze within the enclosure, while two hundred painted savages, clad in white robes with fancy trimmings, move slowly around in a circle, keeping time with a wild chant that swells and falls in barbaric cadence, while two hundred more stand or crouch around the fires, waiting their turn to participate.

"How can I describe this new step of the ghost dance? It is like a military side step to the left accompanied by an indescribable movement of the body. All the dancers face toward the center holding each other's hands and all join in the chant. The dust issued in clouds from beneath two hundred scraping feet, and what with dirt and exertion the dancers are soon exhausted and drop out, while others take their places" (Miller 1952: 333-4).

The "favorite mode of painting" in this graphic and perhaps overly colorful description might mean that most individuals were painted in one way, but that others, perhaps special functionaries, were painted differently. The reporter, however, does record that white clothing was demanded of the dancers, that a windbreak was erected, and described after his own fashion the Pai ghost dance adaptation of the typical American Indian round dance. The account continues:

"They dance until the circle has gone completely around, then stop for a few minutes and rest, then start up again. At each new start they sing a different chant, and so the dance goes on until midnight, when with a loud clapping of hands, they break ranks and go home. During all this time two or three chiefs or medicine men moved around outside the circle preserving order and reprimanding any merriment or hilarity. Chief Ko-ar-a explained that this was a religious dance and that due solemnity must be observed" (Anonymous 1892: 66). [The text varies in the two reprinted versions; the latter was condensed by Mooney (1896: 814-5).]

The description of the 1891 dance differs in certain respects from that of the 1889 performance. The earlier account reported an all-night dance ending with the dancers bathing in the spring, while the later record has the dance ending at midnight. Thus, we have evidence either that the form of the Pai ghost dance changed in this respect during those two years, or that the Anglo-American observers' perceptions differed either absolutely or because they witnessed different phases of the dance cycle.

Degree of Ceremonial Intensity

Mekeel was not sure, on the basis of his informants' descriptions, how long a ghost dance lasted, or how often one was performed. He thought that performances ranged "from several in a month" to "one

[6]

or two months" apart. The most precise mention is of a total of "seven four-night dances at forty-day intervals in different places" (Kroeber 1935: 199). Such a degree of formal scheduling appears to us to be inconsistent with the loose structuring of Pai ceremonialism. Old Mike's 1929 account of the first dance at Grass Springs does give a clearer time picture than Mekeel's summary would suggest.

"They waited for the next dance. All the men went out hunting jackrabbits and cottontails. In five days Jeff spoke again and told them, 'Clean yourselves, wash your clothes. You must be clean. If you don't get clean, our relatives who have died will not come.'

"The next day, the sixth day, the men brought fire wood with teams. At night they started to dance. This was in the fall when it was getting cold. All the young girls and boys danced as they had before and the older people watched. Before midnight they stopped dancing. And the leader, Jeff, went out into the darkness. When he came back he told the dancers that he had heard the ghosts speaking to him. He heard them crying to him, 'The dance is good; it looks fine. If you do this two or three years, your relatives will come back alive.'

"This was continued for fourteen days, quitting at midnight every night. On the fifteenth day they kept dancing all night. Jeff told the crowd, 'This looks fine; I hear the ghosts saying not to stop dancing.'

"They danced for two months, and then the crowd said to Jeff, 'Our food is nearly gone. We have nothing to eat. How can we dance?' But Jeff said to them, 'We are going to dance for one month more.' They began another dance. In one moon they all quit. They had nothing more to eat; they were all out of flour, sugar, and coffee" (Kroeber 1935: 200).

Old Mike's account indicated that the gathering of Pai at Grass Springs to perform the ghost dance stayed together some four months, performing a series of dances of varying length.

Newspaper notices of the time provide some corroboration for the long duration of the encampment and the dancing. An article the following year on later dances remarked that "This dance made its first appearance among the Wallapais in May of 1889" (MCM Nov.

[7]

29, 1890). If accurate, this statement reflects later knowledge gained from the Indians, for the first notice *at the time* appeared in the first week of August (MCM Aug. 3, 1889). Two weeks after the first published reference to the Grass Springs dance, the *Miner* commented on the encampment's shortage of food: "They are getting short of provisions and a number of deaths have occurred from lack of food, and if the foolishness lasts the time allotted the number of good Indians will be largely increased" (MCM Aug. 17, 1889). By the first week in September, the Anglo-American settlers in aboriginal Pai territory were seriously disturbed by the Indians' actions.

> "These Indians about two months ago went up to Grass Springs to meet the other tribes of the Territory [Arizona], when a big pow-wow was inaugurated, which is still going on full blast. Settlers in that vicinity say that the Indians are being incited to marauding by the Piute medicine men, and numerous complaints of cattle killed are being made" (MCM Sept. 7, 1889).

By this time, the lack of provisions was evidently leading the Pai, under the stress of hunger, to kill Anglo-American livestock.

Viewed in light of these contemporary records of the summer start of the 1889 ghost dance, the question arises as to the accuracy of Old Mike's recall in 1929. When he placed the wood-gathering of the sixth ceremonial day in the fall, was he rationalizing the need for firewood to provide light for the dance as a need for warmth?

Not all Pai participated in the ghost dance with the same degree of intensity. As might have been expected on the basis of their previous post-conquest experiences, these Indians took part in the movement in accordance with different stages of acculturation and attitudes toward Anglo-Americans among the various extended kindreds. While the enthusiastic adherents to the cult danced at Grass Springs, the kinship units led by Walapai Charley and Leve Leve (the principal accommodationist leaders) camped near Kingman, although they may have been wavering in their resistance to the appeal of Indian magic. The same newspaper issue last cited reported that "the Indians near Kingman have for the past two weeks been making the night hideous with their 'sings' and 'cries'. . ." or mourning rituals. Many other Pai

Walapai Charley, Walapai leader and early skeptic of the Ghost Dance. Photo by George Wharton James, ca. 1895, courtesy Southwest Museum.

were still not gathered at Grass Springs as a newspaper two weeks later made clear.

"The various bands of the Wallapais are holding a dance and powwow at Grass Springs, seventy-five miles northeast of Kingman, and the various bands were ordered to assemble there last week. Portions of the bands did not attend and the absentees were sent for by the medicine men, who demanded their attendance immediately under penalty of death from a shower of hail-stones which the medicine men would cause to fall on them. The Indian who had refused to go on receiving this summons left immediately. The sudden disappearance of the Indians from their usual haunts alarmed the whites in the vicinity of Hackberry and Peach Springs, and they instantly came to the conclusion that they intended going on the war path . . ." (MCM Sept. 21, 1889).

The fears of the settlers that the Pai were preparing for war led several braver souls to venture into the ghost dance encampment to discover what actually was going on, with the result that the *Miner* published information derived from persons who actually saw the dance. "In order to fully satisfy everybody's fears J. H. Johnson and John Kolar went to the Indians' camp at Grass Springs on Sunday and returned Tuesday evening to Hackberry to inform the people of the situation," the paper reported on Sept. 28, 1889. This was the last reference to the ghost dance published in the *Miner* during 1889, indicating that the long-continued encampment at Grass Springs broke up soon after, or else the settlers lost interest.

After this initial long emotional splurge, lasting from May into late September, the Pai evidently settled down to a shorter form of the ghost dance. This may have been a move to bring the ceremonial into balance with food resources, or to emulate the basic Paiute ceremonial period. The precarious post-conquest economy may have reduced the Pai to the limitation of ritual gatherings of 300 persons to six days that obtained among the Shoshone (Harris 1940: 53), or this pattern simply followed the ghost dance movement ritual periods.

In 1891, at any rate, Chief Sherum, Coara, and a shaman told a *Miner* correspondent: "Each dance lasts five nights and the last night we dance until morning" (Miller 1952: 334; Anonymous 1892: 66).

Molly Mulgullo, one of the authors' Havasupai respondents, who witnessed a Ghost Dance performance in her canyon village. Photo by R. C. Euler, 1959.

Most of the published references to the dance among the Pai follow this *Miner* eyewitness. An independent investigation about the same time suggests that practice may have varied, since the commander at Ft. Whipple was informed in the fall of 1890 that, "each dance lasted four or five nights in succession" (Mooney 1896: 814). The Pai perhaps deviated occasionally from the original Paiute pattern of dancing five nights as preached by Wovoka, the "prophet" of the ghost dance movement (Mooney 1896: 772, 814). The first-hand newspaper descriptions of the Pai ghost dances published from 1889 on indicate that many Pai joined the movement with a fervor that lasted all summer in the first year. On the other hand, these records also reveal that not all Pai were converted, and that the length of the ghost dance ceremonies was reduced in later years to correspond to the Pai capacity to accumulate an economic surplus under post-conquest conditions that seriously restricted their productivity, but brought them U. S. government rations.

Vision Trance Aspect

One of the features of the ghost dance as performed among the Pai clearly demonstrates the psychological significance of the cult. This was the induction of a trance through physical exhaustion, a trance in which visions were seen. This is the principal symptom of "total conviction" which Mead (1959: 326-7) regards as a worldwide phenomenon and which various sources have described for the Pai.

As Mekeel wrote: "Only some people saw the spirits of the dead, apparently outside the dance circle. They fell unconscious and were laid by the pole until they recovered. Some were seized with tremblings. Those who had become unconscious told of their 'dream' (trance vision)" (Kroeber 1935: 199).

The best descriptive evidence of this pattern of behavior comes from an account written by a participant-observer in a Cataract Canyon dance led by a Chemehuevi missionary. There, women were "very often" affected by an "excitement" that he compared to that of Negroes at revival meetings. They followed two patterns. "With a shriek, the woman hysterically leaps within the circle made by the dancers, and howls and shouts and dances and jumps, and then, perhaps, throws herself in a heavy stupor upon the ground." Alternatively, "some will run to the center post, and, hanging on with one or both hands, will swing rapidly around until they fall exhausted." Men carried them out to the fires to be attended by other women. This participant-observer reported seeing "three women almost simultaneously" yield to "this uncontrollable frenzy for an hour or longer" (James 1903: 252-255).

Our Havasupai informants reported that "the dancers act like drunk — pass out by pole — then they really died — maybe they were witched" (authors' field notes).

This phenomenon of total conviction was also commented on at the time by newspaper writers:

> "The dancers . . . dance until they become exhausted in which condition they are supposed to see visions, which they relate to the chief on coming to. Chief Surrum says, that on a recent occasion, when he was in a trance the 'Christ' put 'two bits' in his pocket and Surrum is now on a trip to Nevada to consult the Piute medicine men about the matter" (MCM Nov. 29, 1890).

The importance of the vision trance aspect of the ghost dance seems to be attested to by the consistency among the various types of sources mentioning it.

Chapter Two

ACCEPTANCE BY THE PAI

THE GHOST DANCE, of course, was not a traditional Pai ceremony. At the time of its 1870 diffusion, the Southern Paiute and the Pai were apparently not on friendly enough terms for the cult to be communicated from north to south. Friction between the two groups was fostered by the U. S. Army commander of the Upper Colorado subdistrict, who reported that he sent to Ft. Mohave on Oct. 29, 1867, a Paiute chief named Varanap "who I had succeeded in getting to accompany me for the reasons that I would be sure of no outbreak from them while absent, that I wished to get them in hostility with the Hualapais, whose Country adjoins theirs, separated by the Colorado River . . ." (U. S. Senate 1936: 32). The importance of the 1870 ghost dance among the Southern Paiute was, moreover, apparently minimal, if it reached them.

A generation later, however, Paiute-Pai relations had become quite peaceful and probably frequent after Anglo-Americans subdued both groups. Ideal conditions existed for the spread of the second wave of ghost dancing from its Paiute originators to the Pai. Of this, as of the earlier cult, it can be said that: "The early manifestations consisted largely of doctrinal stress on the return of the dead and the end of the world, which in some vague supernatural manner would entail the elimination of the white people." Converts believed these changes imminent (DuBois 1939: 1).

The Pai acquired their ghost dance and its ideology from Southern Paiutes shortly after its revival by Wovoka in Northern Paiute territory. "The ghost dance was introduced from the Paiute of St. George and St. Thomas in 1889, 'two years after the railroad came through' Kingman in 1887" wrote Mekeel (Kroeber 1935: 198). His reconstruction of the date is confirmed in newspaper accounts at the time. "This dance made its first appearance among the Wallapais in May of 1889. The old chief Surrum being the first convert, and the Paiute medicine men

[14]

Pai shamans such as Pagatacoba exerted strong influence in the acceptance of the Ghost Dance. Photo by George Wharton James, ca. 1895, courtesy Southwest Museum.

[15]

conferred the rights of the 'ghost dance,' and the first dance of the tribe was held at an isolated point, called Grass Springs . . ." (MCM Nov. 29, 1890).

The introduction of the cult among the Pai may actually have been due to Paiute missionary effort. Mooney recorded that a Paiute from southern Utah was "inciting" the Hualapai "to dance for the purpose of causing hurricanes and storms to destroy the whites and such Indians as would not participate in the dances." This was, at least, what the commanding officer of Ft. Whipple was told in September of 1890. At that time, ghost dances had been held "for several months," with "a large portion of the tribe" taking part. Each dance reportedly lasted four to five successive nights. This Paiute missionary was reported to be one of a group that "inaugurated the Ghost Dance among the Wallapai the preceding year" (Mooney 1896: 814).

According to Mekeel, "The Paiute leader mentioned as influential in its spread was Panama'ita or Panamo'ita; the Walapai, Doinhu'ka or Jeff, a shaman." Jeff died during the sojourn of the Laboratory of Anthropology field party in 1929. "Jeff took Panamita among the Walapai, and then a party of prominent Walapai including Jeff and several recognized chiefs went to St. George and witnessed the dance" (Kroeber 1935: 198). In the words of Kuni, one of the Laboratory of Anthropology's 1929 informants:

"Djinpuka, Jeff, went to the Ghost Dance. Tamnada went. Oava'dima, my father Kua'da, Levi-Levi, Serum, these four went as far as St. Thomas. The dance was held at St. George. They went there the next night. Sticks were put around in a circle. People danced in a circle around a pole. The dance stopped the fourth morning. Jeff and Tamnada learned all their songs. They had to go a little way from the dancing place, and then the spirits would arrive and say, 'You have done your part as you were ordered. Keep this up for two years and all the dead will return.'

"This didn't come true because people didn't live up to the rules" (Kroeber 1935: 201).

Jeff's role is still well-remembered among his people. "Indian Jeff somehow got in the Paiute country and understood from them that if they danced like that the dead people would come back to life. That was the cause of their getting together. A few Paiutes attended" (authors' field notes). By 1952-57, we were unable to obtain from Pai respondents, even those who participated in ghost dances as youngsters, nearly as much detail about the diffusion of the cult as the 1929 investigators recovered from informants who had been old enough to perceive and remember the mechanisms of transculturation. Old Mike related other details about this innovation as remembered in 1929:

> "One of the Paiute leaders whose name was Panamoita visited Jeff at Duncan ranch, tanyaka'. Jeff took this leader around among the Walapai, and they told them about the dance and urged them to do the same as the Paiute. He said that this dance was for bringing the dead relatives to life. Three times they thus told all the people at monthly or bi-monthly intervals" (Kroeber 1935: 199).

Then Indian Jeff spent a month traveling about advising his tribesmen of the dance to be held at Tanyika.

> "At this time, Kingman was small, and the Walapai were living across from the Commercial Hotel. They filled up all the flat. Before the month had passed they began to travel away on horseback. They camped at the mouth of Canyon Station, Waikai-ila. Next morning they traveled again and reached a place called Kisia'lva. They were going slowly and camped in that place. This party included the whole Kingman camp, except Walapai Charlie who remained. The next day they came to Tanyaka in the evening. There were gathered all the Walapai from all the divisions. But Mapat was not there, nor Walapai Charlie" (Kroeber 1935: 200).

Newspaper articles contemporary with the event make it clear that more than just two individuals stayed away from the Grass Springs dance. "The bands of Leve Leve and Wallapai Charley, who have their camps about this place, refuse to take part in the dance, and they are awaiting the fulfillment of the medicine men's prophecy of the hailstorm which will kill alike the whites and the disobedient Indians" (MCM Sept. 21, 1889). In this instance, the reporter was certainly capable of observing and talking to those Indians who remained in Kingman and he obviously was acquainted with the ghost dance beliefs. As Mekeel wrote, "Several of the Walapai, including Chief

[17]

Charlie, remained skeptical, but others were convinced, and even now attribute the failure of the dead to return to mistakes made in the performance of the dances or to their premature discontinuance" (Kroeber 1935: 198-9).

The first awareness of Kingman newspaper writers of any ghost dancing among the Pai apparently came just before Aug. 3, 1889 when the *Miner* reported that "The Wallapai Indians this week departed for Grass Spring some seventy-five miles north-east of Kingman, there to have a grand pow-wow, which Surrum, the chief, says will last one month" (MCM Aug. 3, 1889). The nature of the movement was, however, still not understood by the Anglo-Americans, for the article went on with a prediction that "The Navajoes, Supais, Moquis, Utes, and Chimeueves will have representatives there. They will have a big rain sing and dance and expect to bring rain in plenty . . . they will probably gamble as long as they can rustle grub in that section and they have anything to win or lose."

Two weeks later, reporters evidently had talked to some of the Indians and learned the true character of the ceremonies. "Wallapais who have returned from Grass Springs say that a 'ghost dance' in which all the tribes took part, all dressed in white and which lasted five days and nights, was had last week and it took all the dance out of the Indians." Then the *Miner* went on to explain the origin and beliefs of the movement:

> "The Piutes are responsible for the gathering of the various tribes at Grass Springs. The medicine men of that tribe say that the Great Spirit told them to gather all the good Indians at that place and that sometime during two moons the Hicos [*i.e., haikoo,* the Pai word for Anglo-Americans] would be totally wiped from the face of the earth by some pestilence and they would become possessors of all the land again. These medicine men keep apart from the rest of the Indians and claim to be in direct communion with the Great Spirit and have a great influence over all those assembled . . ." (MCM Aug. 17, 1889).

Significantly, in talking with the newspaper writer, the Pai placed the recovery of their land at the heart of their concept of the ghost dance movement. The purpose of the whole ceremonial gathering at

[18]

Grass Springs was to bring on the storm or pestilence that would kill off the Anglo-American invaders, so that the Pai would again become possessors of all their aboriginal lands.

A somewhat later summary of the ghost dance ideology in the *Miner* repeats the essential points: "The Walapais are thoroughly imbued with the idea of the coming of Christ, and that the day is not far distant when the Indians will have 'full possession and that all the dead Indians, deer, antelopes and other game will come back,' as one of the Wallapais expressed it" (MCM Nov. 29, 1890). Again the Indians are described as anticipating the disappearance of the Anglo-Americans as the means to their dual goal of full possession of their lands and the restoration to those lands of dead Indians and game animals.

Thus the majority of the Pai were not yet looking forward to wider participation in the material benefits of the industrial society as in "cargo cult" behavior. They, like other ghost dancing Indians (Mair 1959: 133), wanted to return to the good days gone by. The loss of their land base and access to its resources was the primary cause of a psychological state in which the Pai grasped at the ghost dance as a form of compulsive magic to retrieve these former assets and the lifeway that went with them.

Pai Factionalism Under Stress

The ghost dance movement never achieved what could be considered an effective revitalization function that altered the mazeways (Wallace 1956: 266) of all Pai, even briefly. Even at its peak, the movement failed to win the whole-hearted adherence of Pai bands committed to rapid cultural change toward the behavioral models posed by Anglo-Americans. Some Pai individuals, in an instance of anticipatory socialization (Merton 1957: 265), seem to have preferred Anglo-American to Paiute as a reference group for the future. After all, the Paiute had been almost as ignominiously defeated by the whites as had the Pai themselves. Even the most fervent Pai ghost dance leaders displayed a curious overt subservience toward the very Anglo-Americans whose destruction they so avidly sought by magical means. When settlers Johnson and Kolar visited the ghost dance encampment at Grass Springs in 1889 . . .

"They reached the Indian camp at sundown Monday, and the

[19]

dance was going on; but when the object of their visit was explained to Chief Surrum the dance was stopped and a talk was had. Surrum assured Messrs. Johnson and Kolar that the Wallapais had done nothing to excite the fears of the whites, and they would have held their dance nearer the railroad if grass and water could have been as readily obtained . . ." (MCM Sept. 28, 1889).

At this time, according to the same newspaper writer, "the bands of Leve-Leve and Wallapai Charley do not believe in the dance and will not take part in it." He predicted that "In a few days the gathering will disperse and the various bands return to their old haunts." The consequence of Pai factionalism that limited adherence to the ghost dance movement in 1889 and subsequent years lingered in Pai memory until 1929 (Kroeber 1935: 198-99) and certain echoes of bitterness could still be discerned in the 1950's, diversification in modern religious affiliations aside.

Perhaps old Chief Sherum gave Johnson and Kolar some idea of ghost dance ideology similar to that he and Koara and the shaman gave to a *Miner* correspondent two years later:

"We believe in the existence of a powerful Deity, who will come upon the earth sometime within the next three or four years in the form of an Indian. This being is called in the Paiute language, No-ta Win-nup, and this name has been adopted by the other tribes. When No-ta Win-nup comes, all Indians who have died in the ages that are gone will be restored to life and perpetual youth.

"Those who are now old, sick or lame will also be restored. Simultaneously will reappear the game that has existed in past ages, while the white people and all other races, except the American Indian, will perish. Upon Indians who dare to entertain or express a doubt of the truth of these things, the medicine men threaten to bring the most dire and fatal punishments. Each dance is ordered by No-ta Win-nup, who appears to the medicine men on the fifth night of each dance and tells them when to hold the next, and other things which he wishes his people to know . . . Just before daylight the medicine men go up on top of the little butte and talk with the No-ta Win-nup, and upon returning, report his

[20]

sayings to the people . . ." (Miller 1952: 334; Anonymous 1892: 66).

The supernatural sanctions implied by the ghost dance theology, plus the positive goals of removing the Anglo-Americans from Indian lands and bringing back to life the deceased Indians were effective in spreading the cult through the Pai tribe. What other doctrinal points the millenial prophecy set forth the records do not report, beyond the restoration of the game and punishment of Indian skeptics. Very likely there were additional moral teachings (*cf.* Mair 1959: 128-31) which were of less concern to Anglo-Americans and so were not recorded by Anglo reporters.

Some time between September, 1889 and June, 1890, a large ghost dance may have been held near Kingman which went unreported in the local newspaper. On the flat just below the road fork to Stockton Hill, according to one of our informants, "all the Walapais from all parts of their country got together for the biggest dance they ever had, after the white people came. I came from the other side [of Grand Wash Cliffs] to attend. The first dance here was led by Indian Jeff because something like a spirit in heaven came into his life to do this dance so his dead relatives would come alive. That's the way it came to his sense. A different way of performing the dance came direct to Jeff. The Paiute way of dancing it was different" (authors' field notes).

We date this dance during the winter of 1889-90 because it was held here rather than at Grass Springs and thus could not have been the initial performance. Yet this dance, we think, preceded the one at *Ha'a Meté* which occurred in the summer of 1890, on which occasion rasping sticks were first introduced. Rasping sticks were not used by the Pai during the ceremony held on the edge of the valley below Stockton Hill.

On June 28, 1890, the *Miner* reported that: "The Wallapai tribe are about all now at the ranch of Thompson Bros., at Coara Springs, holding a grand dance. The Indians received their last rations for the season on the 16th inst . . ." Apparently the same dance or series of dances continued for at least two months, for on August 23, the same newspaper recorded:

"The Wallapai Indians are having a grand dance near Thompson Bros.' ranch. It is similar to the one held last year at Grass Spring, and a number of piutes are in attendance. The Indians dance and sing until they are completely exhausted, and eight deaths have occurred from over-exertion. This may put a stop to the foolishness, as a good many of the tribe are returning here, although the dance was to have been continued another moon."

This is evidently the dance referred to by the Pai now as having occurred after the dance near Stockton Hill. It was held beside a small hill west of *Ha'a Meté*. "When they danced, they were asking for their dead to come back to life, because they were told by the Paiute Indians that if they danced like that the dead would come back. Those Paiutes had that cut stick [rasping stick] and rested it on top of a pan and worked with another stick, and with it sang. Then these Indians learned that and did that. Three Paiute Indians came here" (authors' field notes).

This series of dances, or a later one, was still going on as late as the first week in December. "Speaking of Surrum reminds us that the Wallapai quij-a-tee [ghost] dance is still in full blast at Wat. Thompson's ranch and the MINER staff is cordially invited to attend . . . as Jesus Christ is expected to be in attendance almost any night it would be well for those who attend to come on burros," wrote the Kingman paper's Mineral Park correspondent (MCM Dec. 6, 1890).

Meanwhile, the Indians who had refused to join in the Grass Springs observance of the ghost dance the previous year had succumbed somewhat to their anxieties engendered by the conflicting social pressure from other Indians and from the Anglo-Americans. Those following the leadership of Leve-Leve, on participating in the ghost dancing, did not join the dance going on at *Ha'a Meté*. They staged their own performance.

"The Wallapai Indians are holding another 'ghost dance' in Free's Wash, in Wallapai mountains. The dance is held by Levy-Levy's band, the last band of the tribe to join the Messiah craze. This dance made its first appearance among the Wallapais in May of 1889. The old chief Surrum being the first convert and the Piute medicine man conferred the rights of the 'ghost dance', and the first dance of the tribe was held at . . . Grass Springs . . . The

Kate Crozier, one of the authors' Walapai respondents about the Ghost Dance movement. Photo by R. C. Euler, 1956.

Indians were greatly excited at the time . . . Since then the dances have been held in various parts of the county, by the various bands and, in August of this year, a dance which was attended by all the bands was held near Cora Springs . . . and lasted several weeks . . . The dances result in the death of the dancers, at the August dance, eleven Indians died from exhaustion . . ." (MCM Nov. 29, 1890).

The various references to Chief Sherum show that he played a key role in Pai acceptance of a foreign ceremonial much like that of Robert Yellowtail, superintendent of the Crow reservation, when he encouraged socially peripheral Crows to learn a Shoshone version of the Sun Dance (Voget 1948: 640).

This gathering at Free's Wash apparently continued during the winter into 1891. Late in January, Walapai Charley "sent out messengers to inform the ghost dancers of the issuance of rations on Sunday, but on their return they refused to tell anything that Sherum said or what he intends to do . . ." (MCM Jan. 24, 1891). Here is continuing evidence that Charley had not yet joined the cult. Then, on February 7, the *Miner* reported that: "The fact is that Sherum and all the Indians of the Wallapai tribe who can be induced to join him are giving a terpsichorean performance near Free's Wash and but two Indians of the Yava Supai tribe are among them."

Transmission to Eastern Bands

The western Pai seem to have had little success in persuading the Mohave to join in the ghost dance movement. It was, however, transmitted to the Chemehuevi, whether by their linguistic affiliates, the Southern Paiute, or by the Pai cannot be ascertained. Again, the *Miner* reported the event:

"The Messiah craze has at last struck the Chimihuava tribe. They are now holding a ghost dance in the Colorado river valley below Ft. Mohave. The Mohave Indians, who do not believe in the Messiah, have ordered the dancers to leave the valley and go to the mountains with their dance. A number of Wallapai warriors and gazelle-eyed maidens mounted upon coal cars left Tuesday for the scene of the ceremonies. The MINER is in direct telegraphic communication with the High Priest of the Indian Mes-

Chief Navajo, Havasupai leader during the Ghost Dance period. Photo by George Wharton James, 1898, courtesy Southwest Museum.

siah and will keep its readers posted upon the movements of that being and will notify them in advance when the day of destruction will arrive" (MCM Dec. 12, 1891).

The western Pai, however, succeeded in passing the belief and practice on to the eastern Havasupai bands at least for a brief time. Early in 1891, a delegation from Havasupai headed by Chief Navajo visited the Pai performers in the west, and took back the theory and practice of ghost dancing to their canyon village where some Havasupai embellishments were apparently added. Perhaps Chief Navajo was one of the Havasupais noted at the performance at Free's Wash in February.

Some information about the eastern band performance comes from Hopi traders who witnessed the ceremony in Cataract Canyon and who were interviewed by A. N. Stephen and Thomas V. Keam. One Hopi told Keam of his experiences at one performance in Cataract Canyon, which indicate the consistency in form of the spreading cult rituals. As the Hopis approached the "Cohonino camp," they were met by a Havasupai who informed them that his fellow tribesmen were all "engaged in a very important ceremony." The traders were told that "they must wash their bodies and paint them with white clay" before they could go into the encampment, showing the diffusion to the eastern bands of the theme of ceremonial cleanliness. When the Hopis had complied, "they were escorted to the camp." There they were "introduced to the principal chief and headmen, all of whom they found engaged in washing their heads, decorating themselves, and preparing for the ceremony, which took place on a clear space near the camp late in the afternoon . . ." (Mooney 1896: 813). The Hopi traders watched the dance and later told Keam about it:

"During this night dance a long pole, having a tail of an eagle fastened to its end, was brought and securely planted in the ground, and the dancers were told by some of their shamans that anyone who could climb this pole and put his mouth on the tail would see his dead mother or his maternal ancestors. One man succeeded in climbing it and laid his mouth on the feathers, and then fell to the bottom of the pole in a state of collapse. They deemed him dead, but before dawn he recovered and then told

[26]

that he had seen his dead mother, father, and many other ancestors who told him they were all on their way back . . ." (Parsons
1936: II: 996; this is the same as Stephen's letter in Mooney 1896:
831).

Keam elicited from the Hopi trader Putci information that the man
who climbed the pole was revived by the medicine men, and that the
ceremony lasted four days, with the whole village participating (Mooney 1896: 814).

Our Havasupai band informants referred to this dance in the Cataract Canyon village as the first they had held and one elderly woman
who observed it believed that it had been transmitted to them directly
from the Southern Paiute. Once again, recent informant statements
about the process of ghost dance diffusion do not agree entirely with
the evidence in the published record, since the effective mode of
learning the ritual by the Havasupai was almost certainly participation
in the Free's Wash rites of the western Pai.

Only a few dances were held in the main Havasupai village, but during the winter months until *circa* 1892-3, some were held on the plateau above the village. Our informants listed two separate locations in
the higher country where ghost dancing was performed and upon at
least one occasion, "two Paiute from near Tuba City came and sang
every night." One of these areas was at *Hwal'kawá* (Sheep Tank),
a short distance southwest of Grand Canyon; the other was at
Wyov'Koté (Black Tank), north of Ash Fork.

Not all Havasupai participated, however, and some who did not
thought that the others had been bewitched. "A few years later they
quit it" (authors' field notes).

We have only superficial evidence that the ghost dance, or remnants
of it, might have lasted longer among the eastern Pai bands. In an
anonymous account published in 1899, it was reported that an agent
to these Indians saw such a dance *circa* 1895:

"Superintendent McCowan says he was a spectator at one of
these [annual religious] ceremonies, but did not sit the pro-
gramme through. The participants kept up a monotonous but
energetic action, circling about a pole, to which was attached some
'medicine.' A chief kept spurring them on, and as they fell from

exhaustion they were dragged from the ring and fresh dancers took their places" (Anonymous 1899).

The ghost dance did not seem to have any more lasting hold on the Havasupai, possibly because it was already losing its hold on the western Pai bands at the time they learned it.

"It was practiced only one year, being discontinued because they did not like it. All the men who climbed the pole died soon after. At that time, they heard of a Paiute shaman, named Pana-manta . . . living near St. George, Utah, who preached the doctrine that the dead, who had instructed him to so inform the people, were to return to life" (Spier 1928: 266).

A more contemporaneous account confirms direct missionary effort among the Cataract Canyon dwellers, and casts doubt on the claim that the movement endured only a single year there. An Anglo-American took part in a dance in Cataract Canyon when a "Cheme-huevi Indian who was to be director of the music of this religious festival" preached fervently that the recent deaths from influenza were due to the Havasupai having "laughed too much, gone hunting and visiting white men's camps when they ought to have been danc-ing" (James 1903: 249). The observer labeled this man an "evangelist," praising his musical ability. After each exhortation, he "sang out, line for line, a new song that he desired them to learn. At first he alone sang, then Navaho and a few of the older ones took up the strain, and soon all joined in" (James 1903: 255).

Our own informants believed that the ghost dance movement had a two to three year duration among the Havasupai. A government teacher who worked at the Cataract Canyon village near the turn of the century thought that the vision trance aspect of the ghost dance may have been retained in more traditional Havasupai rituals (Iliff 1954: 180).

The eastern bands, especially the Havasupai in their relatively iso-lated area, had not been subject to the same intensity of contact-produced stress that had struck the western Pai. This fails to account for their apparently longer belief in and practice of the ghost dance cult than the western bands, if the degree of intensity of millenial behavior is proportional to the amount of psychological deprivation, as

[28]

implied by Nash (1955:378, 439-42), who showed that those sections of the Klamath Reservation that suffered most from Anglo-American contact had the most aggressive fantasy content during the 1870 ghost dance.

Chapter Three

END OF THE GHOST DANCE MOVEMENT

THE HYPOTHESIS has been advanced that the abandonment of the ghost dance response to stress correlates with the resort to direct aggression against members of the dominant white group (Nash 1955: 438). This hypothesis implies that the use of force and fantasy behavior are mutually exclusive. After noting that the Sioux did not lose interest in the ghost dance when they left their reservation in 1898 in a prelude to massacre, Mair (1959: 120) noted that the content of such movements could not be evaluated. She cited a data problem, asserting that it was impossible to follow the course of such a Utopian movement "to its natural conclusion." Because subject peoples carry on these cults in the presence of the same dominant group against whom the fantasy aggression is directed, the latter demand that their forces of law and order crush the movement. "People who are aware that their destruction is being promised to enthusiastic audiences are not often calm enough to derive assurance from their own disbelief in miracles," she points out. Not often, perhaps, but at times they are. The Anglo-American population of Mohave County in 1889 and immediately subsequent years was, indeed, calmly skeptical of miracles, and particularly those wrought by Indian magic. The dominant group in contact with the Pai regarded the whole messianic movement as plainly ridiculous, as the tone of the reports in the *Miner* reveals. Although the settlers were briefly frightened when the Pai began to ghost dance, it was only because they feared Pai resort to force. As soon as they found that the messianic message was magical, they forgot their fears. As a result, they never employed force against the Pai ghost dancers who were able, therefore, to pursue its course to a "natural conclusion." That conclusion we now wish to describe, since it lends particular theoretical interest to the Pai ghost dance history.

The ghost dance cult among the Pai passed its peak and began to lose adherents in the spring of 1891. There was an immediate reason

[30]

for the reversal of the trend when the leaders of the cult attempted a demonstration of their life-restoring powers, recorded at the time in the local newspaper:

"Old Sherum, head war chief of the Wallapais, in company with one of his lieutenants, is on a visit to the Piutes near Utah. He has gone to consult with the medicine men of that tribe in regard to his ghost dances which of late have begun to lose interest for his savage fanatics, despite his visions of 'happy hunting grounds,' beautifully adorned; and happy ancestors and their conversation with Sherum and his head medicine man, Pay-sui-ya.

"To keep up the fanatical excitment these two imposters have, of late, been compelled to resort to the most desperate pretexts. About a week ago, an Indian died at Peach Springs and Pah-sui-ya [sic.] undertook to restore him to life. At this instance a tall pole was erected, the dead man placed at its base and then all the Indians who could be collected joined hands and danced around the corpse in a circle, all the while chanting some words taught them by the medicine man. This was kept up until everyone was exhausted and the dead man began to decompose, when he was taken up and cremated. According to the ancient custom of the tribe, the medicine man was branded an imposter and a liar . . ." (MCM April 25, 1891)./

This dramatic incident seems not to have been reported to the Laboratory of Anthropology field party of 1929 by its informants. We were not able to elicit information about it in the 1950's. So this, then, seems to be an example of ethnographic information of key importance in the understanding of the dynamics of rejection of an alternative cultural pattern being recoverable *only* from the news accounts contemporary with the event. Pai memory of the negative experience of ghost dancing seems to have been selectively repressed long ago. Yet the newspaper account indicates that the Pai messianic movement was put to the test, without being suppressed by dominant group force. Thus, the explanation that the rituals could not be carried out because of forceful inhibition (Mair 1959: 132) was not available to the Pai ghost dance leaders, assuming that they themselves wished to carry on. Two dance cycles were even begun apparently immediately

[31]

after the issuance of government rations. The eastern bands reported at the turn of the century that they stopped ghost dancing because some persons who climbed the central pole died a short time afterward (Iliff 1954: 180). Both events were dramatic ones of a nature permitting the Pai to make frequency interpretations (Erasmus 1961: 22-48) that were not favorable toward the movement.

ˋGhost dancing did not stop immediately after the April failure at resuscitation, but enthusiasm appears to have slacked off appreciably.ˊ The *Miner* reported that as soon as the western bands received their ration on May 25th, they planned to "commence their last grand ghost dance. The superstitious fears of the Wallapais are being worked on and nearly all the tribe will be induced to join in what they claim will be their last grand carnival" (MCM May 16, 1891). The day before the ration issue, the newspaper announced that: "The Wallapais will have a grand ghost dance at Grass Springs next week. The dance is to be after the masquerade order, as the participants will have their features and forms wholly concealed" (MCM May 23, 1891).

Ghost dances were also apparently scheduled in the Walapai Mountains for June 11 and July 1 (Anonymous 1892: 66). The end of the 1891 ghost dance season seems to have come early in December:

> "The Wallapai dance at Coara Springs has suspended operations during the cold snap and the dancers are returning to their respective homes. Nota-win-up, the Indian Messiah, is still forcibly detained by the devil, we are informed by the Wallapais, and the whites are still permitted to enjoy this sunny land of Arizona. When Nota-win-up is released from durance vile the Indians say he will carry out his former intention of depopulating the county of whites and restoring the noble redmen to their former grandeur . . ." (MCM Dec. 5, 1891).

In mid-December, the *Miner* announced that: "The Wallapais are going to build a corral on the flat above Kingman, where they will hold their ghost dances in future." The paper also reported that Walapai Charley had been converted to the messianic belief and was taking the lead "in all matters spooky" (MCM Dec. 19, 1891). A week later, the editor reported, however, that "Wallapai Charlie denies that he has been converted to the Messiah belief, but says that he is always willing to take part in the ceremonies of his benighted brethren if there is a good supply of grub on hand" (MCM Dec. 26, 1891).

Acceptance still had not become tribal-wide, for: "A few of the younger and more progressive Indians refuse to believe in these prophecies, or to take any part in the dances" (Anonymous 1892: 67). Before complete acceptance could be accorded the ghost dance cult, it appeared already on the wane. Since Mead (1959: 326) advocated assuming "readiness for conversion" to be "a universal social phenomenon," the steadfast refusal of some Pai to accept the ghost dance doctrine as absolute truth holds some theoretical significance. This refusal suggests the possibility that readiness for conversion is not in fact universal, or at least that readiness for conversion of a given population to a given doctrine at a given time cannot be assumed. The general assumption advanced by Mead may apply to those Pai who consistently rejected ghost dance millenialism. They may not have been open to conversion because they were already committed to some form of European religious belief, or had simply become confirmed skeptics with regard to Indian belief. Certainly there is evidence that Walapai Charley behaved in terms of the latter kind of belief structure, but data on other Pai who were not ready for conversion to the ghost dance cult simply are not available.

Definite signs of decreasing commitment to the messianic movement were reported in the *Miner* the following spring.

> "The Wallapais received their monthly allowance of rations Monday and danced for three or four evenings in honor of the occasion. Their interest, however, in these dances seems to be on the wane, as very few participated and those who did went about it in a half hearted way as though the festivities were becoming decidedly monotonous" (MCM March 12, 1892).

The passage of time did not rekindle the initial enthusiasm of the Pai for the ghost dance. At the end of July . . .

> "Pah Qui-ya, the head medicine man of the Wallapais, was in town the early part of the week rounding up the noble warriors and beautiful maidens of the tribe to attend the first of a series of Ghost Dances now beginning to be inaugurated at Ko-a-ra Springs, or about a half a mile south of it. Owing to the fact that

[33]

his reverence, the High Priest of the Indian Messiah, had much difficulty in securing an attendance on his ceremonies toward the close of the last series that ended in the spring, he has concluded to add a few attractions to the ordinary excitement of ghost dancing by getting up a few horse races, shinny games and other steriotyped [sic.] forms of the 4th of July amusements. Dr. Pah Qui-ya will have to get up some new and original features to his ceremonies if he succeeds in keeping up the interest of the ignorant and excitable savages in his silly orgies" (MCM July 30, 1892).

Later issues of rations to the western Pai bands did not bring comments from the *Miner's* editor about ghost dancing, although he dutifully recorded the issues. On December 10, 1892, "a great number of hungry Indians were on hand for the distribution." On January 14, 1893, "they immediately proceeded to gamble off what they had just received to their visiting Mohave friends from the Colorado river." On February 11, 1893, 10,000 pounds of flour and 18,000 pounds of beef had been issued the day before. March 11, 1893 was another issue date. On November 25, 1893, the *Miner* reported another issue earlier in the week. On December 23, 1893, several fights over rations were reported.

By this time, the messianic message of the ghost dance appears to have fallen largely into discard among the Pai. Mohave County suffered from drought during the summer of 1893, and that great tribal entrepreneur, Sherum, undertook to do something about it:

"Chief Sherum, of the Wallapai, has just returned from an extended trip into the Piute country. He says that a big medicine man of the Paiutes had told him that the Navajos, Supais, Moquis, Chemehuevas, Maricopas, and Apaches were to be told that great rains would soon visit all the lands over which they held dominion if they would believe the predictions of the Piute prophet, but that if they laughed at the voice of the medicine prophet, . . . no rain would fall. He also said that all good Indians must engage in dances and that rains would fall at regular intervals for the next two or three months and that all the Indians would have fat cattle and horses; that the whole country would be covered with grass and good Indians would be living on the fat of the land" (MCM Aug. 26, 1893).

Thus, Sherum appeared still to be seeking supernatural solutions to practical problems, seeing Indian-Anglo-American relations in somewhat more realistic terms, but not returning to merely personal problems only, nor eschewing supernatural intervention as Mair (1959: 132) suggested often occurs following periods of extravagant collective expectations. In the passage quoted above may be discerned, too, the elements of integration of Pai economy with the Anglo-American economy on something other than subordinate wage labor roles for the Pai. They had begun to think in terms of owning cattle and horses, sources of wealth and prestige extremely important to the Anglo-American settlers on the Pai aboriginal range. Eventually, cattle production became very important economically for the western Pai on their reserved lands. By 1916, the local agent of the Bureau of Indian Affairs supervised a tribal herd of 900 head of cattle and 100 horses, and had purchased 150 cows allotted to individual Indians (U. S. Senate 1936: 207).

In August, 1895, another instance of ghost dance cult activity was reported: "The Indians have been ghost dancing at Chloride this week. Old Sherum is working the braves up and is trying to instill a little fighting blood into them" (MCM Aug. 31, 1895). This is the latest reference to Pai ghost dancing we have been able to find. It appears as an isolated incident, possibly mis-identified.

If this was in fact a late attempt at ghost dancing, it indicates that those Pai directly under the authority of Chief Sherum carried on the cult for some six years, not the two years the Walapai participated (Spicer 1962: 273). Nor had the movement "within three years completely died out" as Spicer (1962: 528) concluded from an earlier draft of this study.

Even in discard, the ghost dance movement left at least one tangible and permanent change in northeastern Pai behavior. Having customarily cremated their dead, these Indians reportedly began to bury them in rock slides or cairns, since a corpse could arise from beneath stones more easily than from scattered ashes. Iliff (1954: 266) recorded Havasupai attribution of this change to the Paiute. Later, Christian missionary activity reinforced the change.

[35]

Chapter Four

STRESS AND SUBORDINATION

THE REASONING and emotionalism behind Pai borrowing of the ghost dance from the Southern Paiute can be understood best with reference to the types of dominant group pressures they were under at that time. These pressures have not been discussed in a very systematic manner in previous reports on the Pai. Kniffen's paragraphs on changes of the flora in the area ranged by the western bands (Kroeber 1935: 36) and Mekeel's brief summary of the ghost dance frequently referred to in these pages comprise the total Laboratory of Anthropology field party attention to changes in the situation of western Pai bands from the pre-conquest ways of life reconstructed in its report, except in the commendably reproduced statements by informants. There was no discussion of the mental attitudes of the recently defeated Pai in *Walapai Ethnography*. Although tales of inter-tribal warfare appear in *Havasupai Ethnography* (Spier 1928: 356-74), it, too, neglected post-conquest Anglo pressures. The general types of psychological stress that all Pai bands suffered after 1869 included most of those Leighton (1949: 76-7) recognized as disturbing all peoples. A few examples of the types and amounts of stress to which the Pai were subjected in the late 19th Century will clarify their motivations in ghost dancing.

Life Threats

The aboriginal territory of the Pai varies from quite arid lowlands toward the west to pineclad plateaus on the east. Even the high pine forests are not well watered. Permanent streams are few, so springs and rainwater catchment basins are the keys to human land use (Kroeber 1935: 29-30; Spier 1928: 92) as well as stock grazing over most of the area. The prime need for water quickly brought Anglo-Americans into direct conflict with the Pai following their military conquest. The Pai faced, therefore, direct threats to their lives in attempting to utilize some springs where Anglo-Americans had used force to exclude the Indians and taken possession.

". . . when these cattlemen come in an put their horses and cattle on this water, on this good country range, they told us that was theirs. That is their water, that is their land . . . When these men hire cowmen, you know, in olden days they wear long whiskers and that pistol in their hand right now . . . in those days they were very dangerous . . . These cowmen just had their gun ready, you know, and we were scared of them. And that is why we don't live close to these waters any more then, you know. That is why we moved to other places . . . I remember myself we live on the place where my grandfather used to live . . . we raise garden there in my time . . . this fellow, white man named Frank Miller, he owned cattle and he ranged the cattle in the creek there. And he told us one day — when the sun comes up about here he come up with pistol in his side and a long rifle, and pistol, too. He come up to there and told us to get away from there because the water belonged to him and he water the cattle there, and the ranges belong to him. You know, might harm the cattle going there" (Indian Claims Commission 1950: 75-6).

The reaction of the Anglo-Americans in western Pai country at the time of the first ghost dance ceremonial only twenty years after the military defeat of the western bands illustrates how very close to the edge of direct physical violence these settlers were.

"A petition from the people of Mohave County to General Miles, asking that the commander at Fort Mohave be instructed to investigate the suspicious actions of the Wallapai Indians, was being circulated in Kingman this week . . .

"Sheriff Lake daily receives a number of letters from ranch and cattlemen who are alarmed at their strange actions . . . It is evident that the 'medicine men' have stirred up all the superstitions of which a savage is capable, and if the ways of God are mysterious, the ways of a live Indian are more so.

'Music hath charms to soothe the savage breast . . .'

"And it is said that the most effective is the whistle of a well-directed bullet" (MCM Sept. 7, 1899).

[37]

Thus, the only newspaper to which most of the Anglo residents in the Pai country had access was virtually inciting them to open warfare against the Indians, even though it was in possession of enough facts about the ceremonial going on at Grass Springs to conclude that there was no danger from the Indians.

Health Threats

The Pai also faced threats to their well-being in the form of a number of epidemics of communicable diseases introduced to them by the Anglo-American invaders. Although little analytical use was made of them in the Laboratory of Anthropology field party report, informant statements in 1929 emphasized the seriousness of epidemic disease. One respondent claimed to have dreamed about epidemics of smallpox and whooping cough before they occurred. Another reported gonorrhea as "the most prevalent Walapai disease," with syphilis "prevalent." Since no native "cure" was known for either ill (Kroeber 1935: 117-8), both venereal diseases appear to have been communicated to the Pai population through the exploitation of their women by Anglo-Americans, according to early observers (U. S. Senate 1936: 195). The vaccination of Pai against smallpox apparently began only in 1896 during a chicken pox scare and a measles epidemic (MCM Feb. 18, Feb. 22, Feb. 29, 1896). In the years just preceding the introduction of the ghost dance movement, for example, this was a serious threat to Pai survival. In 1886, the newspaper at Mineral Park reported:

"Several Wallapai Indians have visited the happy hunting grounds in the past few weeks, and have become better Indians than they ever were on earth. They succumbed to a kind of lung fever, which seems to be epidemic among the tribe at this season of the year" (MCM March 21, 1886).

In 1887, the Kingman paper noted that "Surrum, head chief of the Wallapai tribe, is a loser by the measles to the extent of three wives . . ." (MCM June 4, 1887). On January 16, 1892, the *Miner* commented that "A number of Indians have succumbed to the ravages of grip and pneumonia this winter." On March 12, 1892, the same source took note of the death in Albuquerque of two Pai children recently sent to the Indian school there.

Since only especially newsworthy events affecting the subordinate Indian population were reported in this paper, printed by and for Anglo-Americans, it seems safe to infer that the reported incidence of contagious disease and mortality from it was much lower that the actual incidence. One effect of measles, smallpox, gonorrhea and syphilis on Pai health and population trends appears to have been a drastic lowering of the live birth rate as the result of impairment of the reproductive organs of Pai women. This may be reflected in a 1929 informant's statement that "My grandmother said that in the old times she never saw a woman die in childbirth. Nowadays, many die. I have known eleven who died" (Kroeber 1935: 132). Such statements may, of course, reflect a Pai perception of pre-conquest times as a golden age, but the occasional newspaper accounts of infectious epidemics tend to confirm the reality of increased threats to Pai biological survival once they came into steady contact with the reservoir of contagion among the Old World population and its extensions in the western hemisphere.

Differential mortality among Havasupai men and women, Spier suggested (1928: 209), was due to female deaths during childbirth. The sex ratio was 113 men per 100 women as early as 1881 (Coues 1900: II: 345) among the eastern band. It rose steadily to an apparent 145 in 1905 and 151 in 1906, probably as a result of the epidemics mentioned here and others not recorded. By 1919, the sex ratio had dropped back to 124 (Spier 1928: 209-10). The smallness of the population may in itself account for some of this imbalance, but certainly not all of it. Nor can emigration of Havasupai women to marry men from the western bands explain it, since the Walapai showed the same kind of imbalance, although less markedly. In comparison, the Walapai population recorded by the Bureau of Indian Affairs in 1900 had a sex ratio of 108, and in 1906 a ratio of 107.7 (U. S. Senate 1936: 192, 201).

Simply living in contact with Anglo-Americans whose complex industrial economy produced dangerous substances unknown in nature and completely outside previous Pai experience also posed threats to Pai well-being. Examples of such dangers were reported during the ghost dance era. At Kingman . . .

"A little Indian, while playing around Mrs. Ryan's yard, on South Front Street, picked up a bottle of carbolic acid and drank part of the contents. The poor little fellow suffered excruciating pain from the action of the acid in its mouth and throat, but the application of oil seemed to relieve him greatly, and after a few hours he was carried off to the Indian camp. At last accounts, the little one was much better" (MCM May 2, 1891).

Only two weeks later, the local newspaper reported a very similar incident at Stockton Hill mine camp:

"A little Wallapai Indian boy met with a very painful accident at the residence of M. W. Scott. Some very strong amonia had been poured into a teapot for cleansing purposes and Mrs. Scott took it to the water barrel, where she left it, while returning to the house for a cup. During her absence some Indians came up for water and one of the papooses, seeing the teapot took advantage of the opportunity to get a drink of tea. Just as the lady reappeared he was dropping the teapot with a wild yell of pain and fright. In a short time a crowd of squaws had gathered and added their howls and lamentations to the cries of the papoose, until there was a terrific din. The squaws screamed out that he was dying and 'Hicoe's (white people) chi-na-muc-ka (bad) medicine had killed him,' nearly scaring the life out of the boy. Mrs. Scott had her nerves and patience taxed to control and pacify the excited squaws and at the same time administer remedies to the little sufferer. He was finally relieved after unremitting efforts in using several restoratives. He was not able to swallow solid food for several days ..." (MCM May 16, 1891).

Another class of danger posed for the Pai by Anglo society was the death or injury caused by the transcontinental railroad trains.

"A little Wallapai Indian at Peach Spring Thursday, while playing around the cars in the yard at that place, got his hand pretty badly mashed. The switch engine was moving some cars and the little fellow's hand got caught in the car coupler, breaking three of his fingers, and it is probable that his hand will have to be amputated. He was brought to Kingman and the doctor dressed the wounded member and made the little sufferer as comfortable as possible. It is a mystery that more Indian children do not get hurt or killed by the cars as they are eternally jumping on and off

moving trains at this and other points along the line of the road"
(MCM Feb. 25, 1893).

Along with other health threats, the Pai suffered discomfort from
Anglo-American foods to which they were unaccustomed and to which
their digestive tracts had difficulty adjusting, such as milled flour and
coffee beans the Pai did not know how to prepare. While held at Camp
Beale Springs in the early 1870's, Pai women who were accustomed to
a high oil (fat) and low cereal (carbohydrate) content aboriginal
diet "were allowed all the hardtack they could eat, but only on the
most solemn occasions could they gratify their taste for castor-oil —
the condition of medical supplies would not warrant the issue of all
they demanded" (Bourke 1891: 161). Obesity very likely is a post-
conquest phenomenon among the Pai, produced by a shift in diet from
game, seeds, and pit-baked mescal staples to cultivated cereals. A
contemporary newspaper notice of this problem of rations suggested
a remedy indicative of the white settlers' attitude toward the Pai:

> "The Wallapai Indians complain of the quality of the flour
> served out to them by the government, and say it is full of weevils
> and has an intensely bitter taste. A plentiful supply of arsenic
> mixed with it would disguise the bitter taste. We offer this sug-
> gestion to the contractor and sincerely hope he will adopt it"
> (MCM Oct. 8, 1887).

Here certainly is manifested dislike and rejection of the Indians by
the main channel of popular opinion for the Anglo-Americans in immediate contact with the Pai.

Subsistence Threats

In Pai perception, the most serious threat to their lives and health
was probably the obvious loss of their means of gaining subsistence
from their land. Their whole relationship to the land was changing
because of Anglo settlement, farming, and ranching, which excluded
them from their former range. Even the settlers recognized this: "This
is the country of their birth, they know no other, they have no other
place to go. The white man has taken possession of their homes.
Every spring of water is occupied by white men. If they go about it

they are hounded away, because they frighten the stock and drive them from water . . ." (Davis 1882: 3).

In addition, cattle grazing was destroying their vegetable food base. Their own use of fire arms for hunting, combined with that of Anglo-Americans, was depleting their animal food base as well. Thus, the Pai could not continue their individual and collective efforts at food-getting in traditional ways. Even if they wanted to continue, the Pai were forced to idleness or wage labor through loss of their property in land and land resources. Kniffen summarized accurately the floral change in the Walapai country resulting from Anglo settlement:

> "Alterations in the native vegetation effected by the Caucasions are quite obvious when they involve the introduction of agricultural products, or the removal of indigenous species as in lumbering. But there are more subtle changes, particularly affecting the smaller species such as the annuals, which in time may mean the almost complete replacement of the native types . . . it was impossible to obtain a specimen of the much talked of 'sele.' According to Walapai accounts the latter formerly occupied certain valley flats and forest openings almost to the exclusion of other species.

> "Canes or reeds, and something resembling tule, are said formerly to have been abundant about certain sites containing open water . . . The Walapai attribute the disappearance of these hydrophytes to grazing cattle" (Kroeber 1935: 36).

To these plants might be added others such as the water-dependent *ikisa,* a leafy, spinach-like green growing only in constantly soaked soil, which has been grazed to extinction except in a few deep canyon refuge areas. This process of floral and faunal change was recognized by Anglo settlers in the Pai country at a fairly early period:

> "The game is all gone. In 1863 the valleys were filled with antelope and the hills with deer. Rabbits and hares were abundant. Now one may travel for weeks and not see any game save an occasional rabbit. The stock have eaten off the grass so that their harvest fields where they used to gather grass seeds are destroyed" (Davis 1882: 3).

The movements of the Pai were restricted seriously by Anglo-American settlement: by seizure of water sources without which the Indians could not survive in many areas, by chasing them off pre-empted farming and grazing lands, by the use of military force (including physical imprisonment at certain periods), and by the establishment of reservations designed more to keep the Pai off other lands than to keep Anglo-Americans off the reservations. The role envisioned locally for the reserve area in keeping Indians off lands outside its boundaries is stated clearly in an 1885 newspaper article:

"The Indian agent, Mr. C. A. Harvey Jr., informs us that Scherum, chief of the Walapais, has complained to him that Messrs. Robinson and Thompson, have located certain springs, the Kane Spring and others which Scherum claims he has a right to hold. The agent explained to the chief, that the Government had set apart a reservation for the exclusive use of the tribe, and that the whites cannot interfere with the occupancy of the same; and that the balance of the lands formerly occupied by the Indians of his tribe, had, by the Government, been declared open for location and occupancy by the whites. That the land claimed by Messrs. Robinson and Thompson does not lie within the reservation; and that in locating it they but exercise a right given to them by act of Congress. This view of the agent we take to be correct. Mr. Harvey, by a letter which we received on Thursday, informs us that Scherum insists on his right to remain, and has expressed his determination to hold the springs. *Why not send these Indians to the reservation and so avoid these little troubles*" (MCM May 31, 1885; emphasis added).

This policy was hardly reciprocal, however, for despite the agent's statement that the reservation was set apart "for the exclusive use of the tribe, and that the whites cannot interfere with the occupancy of the same," Anglo-Americans actually proceeded to do exactly that, so the Pai in fact possessed not even the secure refuge of an exclusively occupied reserve area.

"The Wallapais have had the same trouble about the white man seizing the best land on their reservation that most other tribes have been subject to. When the reserve was set apart by executive order a man named Spencer was living on land included therein, and he claimed two of the finest springs, one, that of Mattawedi-

[43]

tita, being their most sacred of places. He was soon murdered, whether by Indians or whites I am unable to say, and no one occupied these springs until a man named W. F. Grounds regardless of the executive order, took possession of, and claimed, Mattaweditita to the exclusion of the Wallapais. This he sold to a man named J. W. Munn. Later he and Munn had quarrels about it and both claimed it. Then the Indian Agent interfered, and, finding that the Indians had always claimed it as their own, that it was on their reserve, and that they actually wished to continue to cultivate it, he ordered both men to leave. Grounds had about seventy-five head of cattle and Munn had a garden. The latter vacated quietly, but Grounds brought back his cattle after they were removed. In the meantime the Indians had planted their gardens, and when the cattle came in their crops were speedily demolished. Again the cattle were removed and again brought back. About this time some one generously gave to the Indians, or left where they could be picked up, some melons or cucumbers or both, of which fourteen of the Walapais living in Mattaweditita Canyon partook. Of the fourteen, thirteen sickened and died. Of course there was no way of fastening this dastardly and cowardly crime upon anyone, but whites as well as Indians are pretty generally agreed as to who was its perpetrator" (James 1903: 186-7).

Even the more isolated Havasupai did not escape these threats. A year after the establishment of their separate reservation, the value of the mineral deposits in Cataract Canyon was being touted by John Reese, "practical miner" (AWJ Aug. 17, 1883), an unfortunate being who subsequently fell to his death in the canyon (AWJ Nov. 2, 1883). In 1885, Dr. T. A. Bishop wrote to the Office of Indian Affairs that whites were still invading Cataract Canyon in search of minerals and bothering the Havasupai (Bishop 1885).

About this time, Anglo-Americans began to turn their attentions from mining to the scenic beauties of the Havasupai country, the Grand Canyon in particular. Captain John Hance claimed land on the South Rim on June 15, 1884 (AC Jan. 22, 1887) and by 1886 he was advertising to take tourists and others on excursions into the Grand Canyon (AC Sept. 18, 1886). Anglo-American cattlemen were moving into Havasupai territory in the 1880's also. In fact, a party of Havasupais, apparently not at all understanding the restrictions of their small reservation, ordered cattlemen away from Black Tank, north of Ash Fork, in 1888 (Brayton 1888). A similar incident occurred in 1890 when an Indian, Suppai Tom, wanted "to possess land within the natural limits of a basin known as Rain Tank," south of Grand Canyon, an area which "had been the home of his family for many years." This had been claimed by "two white men and one white woman." The Indian Service official in charge, seemingly uninformed even then as to whether a Havasupai Reservation was in existence, indicated that the Indians had "no right to Rain Tank or any other spot away from said Reservation" (McCowan 1890).

Family Threats

The Pai naturally perceived situations such as these as grave threats to their children and families, even though indirect. There were even more direct and grave threats to Indian families which caused the Pai great stress. Although previous investigators obtained and reported data on pre-conquest marital patterns, they did not concern themselves with the intergroup relations dimension of post-conquest Pai family life. Anglo-American males in old Pai territory became an important influence on Pai families. The Pai women, for example, were often considered fair game by Anglo-American single men in the rough and ready mining camps which formed the backbone of Anglo settlement in the Pai country.

"About seven o'clock . . . it was discovered that Pete Laroque had been shot in the head and instantly killed while asleep in his cot in the corral in the rear of Taggart & Co.'s store. Sheriff Steen, who happened to be in Kingman, was at once notified of the killing and by his orders the body was left undisturbed, while an Indian was sent after the coroner. From information received the Sheriff proceeded to the Indian camp near the sampling works and arrested a Wallapai Indian named 'Dick' and charged him with the murder. He at first denied it strenuously, but finally acknowledged that he was the man who fired the fatal shot, and when asked why he did so said that during the night previous Pete Laroque and a man called Oscar came up to his camp with a couple of bottles of whisky and after getting them all drunk Pete dragged off his

[45]

squaw, while Oscar carried off her sister, that he objected, drunk as he was, and was knocked over the head with a six-shooter by one of the men. That he lay unconscious for a while and as soon as he had recovered sufficiently he procured his rifle and started in search of Pete . . ." (MCM July 27, 1884).

That the Pai were confronted with overt dislike, rejection and ridicule by the whites should be abundantly clear from many foregoing quotations. The settlers' attitude was summed up as "these Indians are a nusance, and an almost intolerable nusance . . ." (Davis 1882: 3).

Unpredictable Authority

On all fronts, the Pai were faced with a superior authority which to their minds was exceedingly capricious and unpredictable, but which was the ultimate determinant of their welfare.

An early example of such behavior by Anglos from the Pai viewpoint was the action of Lt. Col. William R. Price in 1868. This officer, attempting to "pacify" the Pai, required the surrender of Sherum and others leading the Indians, as a condition to the cessation of hostilities. In view of the extent of Price's communication with the Indians, it is impossible that the tribe in general could have known of, or understood this condition. So Price's course of action, quite clear to him, must have appeared utterly capricious to the Indians whom he attacked.

"I have the honor to report that Cherum, the Hualapais Captain, having escaped from the guard while on his way to San Francisco for Confinement, I started from Camp Willow Grove on the 7th inst. with thirty men of Co. E & K of the 8th Cavalry.

"On the morning of the 10th, shortly after daylight in the vicinity of Walker Spring in the Aquarius Range, with 15 dismounted men on a high and rocky mountain, I surprised a Rancheria containing about 20 Indians; killed 3 bucks whose bodies were found, and severely wounded others; captured 3 squaws and 3 children, and destroyed this rancheria . . .

"On the morning of the 13th, surprised another Rancheria containing 5 wickiups, and killed or captured the entire band, killed 8 Indians and captured 7 squaws and 7 children . . ." (U. S. Senate 1936: 79-80).

[46]

Captain John G. Bourke (1891: 161-2) related an incident during the decade immediately preceding the ghost dance movement which well illustrates the confusion in the minds of the Pai as to proper behavior under post-conquest conditions. Captain Thomas Byrne, in command of Camp Beale Spring, had impressed upon the western Pai the importance of notifying him at once of any breach of the peace. One day "Walapai Charlie," a leader in post-conquest Pai adjustment, raced in to report that the white men in Mineral Park had "broken out." Investigation showed that the miners were celebrating a rich strike "in appropriate style," staggering about the camp's single street more or less soberly shooting at the lamps in the two saloons and at one another. As Bourke very accurately summed up the transcultural situation, Charlie "had not yet learned that one of the inalienable rights of the Caucasion is to make a fool of himself now and then." So Charlie ran fourteen frightened miles to inform Captain Byrne of the "outbreak."

The Pai biographies recorded in 1929 contain brief allusions to unpredictable exercise of authority by Anglos, but at a later period in time than that referred to above. Kuni, for example, attributed the deaths of some of his six children who died at school to "a mistake the school doctor made. This killed twenty or twenty-five children" (Kroeber 1935: 208). Another informant remembered losing a job running a mine windlass when the mine closed down after the foreman was shot (Kroeber 1935: 217). The Indian, like many other wage laborers, had no part in the management decision to close down the enterprise for reasons having nothing to do with worker performance.

Chapter Five

REACTION TO DEFEAT

ONE PRIMARY GOAL of the ghost dance movement was the removal
of the stress of land and resource loss by removing the Anglo-Americans
responsible through supernatural means. At first, as the Pai danced at
Grass Springs, "some time during two moons the Hicos would be totally wiped from the face of the earth by some pestilence and they would
become possessors of all the land again" (MCM Aug. 17, 1889). Later,
"the day is not far distant when the Indians will have 'full possession'
. . ." (MCM Nov. 29, 1890).

The other main goal of the ghost dance cult was the restoration of
life to dead Indians. This is evidence that the Pai perceived direct
threats to their lives as the other most disturbing source of stress in
their post-conquest situation. Part of their emphasis on this aspect of
the ghost dance dogma arose, however, from their traditional pattern
of mourning ceremonials and their very real sorrow over the loss of
many relatives at the hands of Anglo settlers and soldiers. When
Sherum said that at the coming of the Messiah, "all Indians who have
died in the ages that are gone, will be restored to life and perpetual
youth. Those who are now old, sick or lame will also be restored" (Miller 1952: 334; Anonymous 1892: 66), he was voicing the Pai response
to immediate conditions under which they lived with very fresh mem-
ories of large numbers of recently killed or deceased relatives.

Even in this concern for the dead, and with the constant direct
threats to life faced by these Indians, the old chief and his fellow
leaders in the ghost dance ceremonials returned to the theme of the
restoration of the land, adding: "Simultaneously will reappear the
game that has existed in past ages . . ." The Indians were aiming their
magic at recovery of ideal subsistence conditions of pre-conquest times
when each family could earn its own living as an independent economic unit utilizing common land resources. The Pai perceived themselves as being poorer than they had been prior to conquest, so that

they must be counted as suffering from deprivation in Aberle's (1959: 79) sense.

When disturbed by stresses such as the Pai were undergoing, "All people have a tolerance-for-stress threshold," according to Leighton. When stresses mount until this threshold is exceeded, people react with some combination of psychological patterns. One pattern is that of effective action aimed at reducing the sources of stress, and another is random behavior. A third pattern is destructive behavior such as suspicion or hostility or hatred, which frequently aims toward substitutes rather than the true sources of stress, and a fourth pattern is simply apathy (Leighton 1949: 77-8). All of these types of response have occurred among the Pai in differing combinations as their tolerance-for-stress threshold has been repeatedly exceeded. Within the psychological patterns of response to great stress must be considered especially important the fantasy pattern, which took the specific ghost dance form of nativistic movement among the Pai, as among other North American Indians.

Military Defeat

In their first contacts with Anglo-Americans, at least some of the Pai correctly viewed the strangers as a direct life threat. Their response was integrated military action along traditional lines to remove the source of stress. They fought to evict the invaders from Pai territory. For example, the explorer Francois Xavier Aubry recorded that on August 3, 1853, while he was in Pai territory, "Indians were around us in numbers all day, shooting arrows every moment. They wounded some of our mules and my famous mare . . ." (Bieber 1938: 362-3).

Other Pai evidently did not conceive Anglo-Americans as a direct threat and carried on peaceful inter-group relations until something happened to cause hostilities. A wagon train emigrant told of such an occurrence in 1858: On the morning of August 20th, "the Indians brought back the horse and mule they had stolen . . ." because they were promised "presents" in return. Members of the train involved "made them presents of blankets, tobacco, clothing and beads, and fed some twenty or thirty of them a day and a night, in the hope that they would molest us no more." This treatment did not secure a peaceful passage for the wagons. The Indians, in the Anglo-American view,

[49]

"wanted some of our oxen and appeared to crave double the value of the animals they had stolen and brought back to us again," lamented one emigrant. The Pai left the wagon train, "apparently in anger," when the emigrants "refused to give them more." After this "first annoyance we had met with from the Indians in our long journey . . . they continued to annoy us from this on . . ." (Udell 1868: 40) to the Colorado River where the Mohaves attacked the advance guard in force and turned the wagon train back.

Meanwhile, after the first misunderstanding that occurred somewhere in the highlands of Pai territory, and by the time the emigrants reached the Cerbat Mountains on August 23rd, "The Indians were frequently shooting their arrows among us, from their hiding places in the rocks and brush, as we passed along, and when in camp, wounding our stock; we were constantly in imminent danger . . ." (Udell 1868: 42).

The beginning of mining operations in Pai country, with the establishment of permanent Anglo-American residences there, probably impressed the Indians as a serious threat to their land resources, and again they reacted by military action against the settlers. "At a mine in Chloride the Indians rushed them, and buried the miners. They got all the white man's guns" (Kroeber 1935: 183).

The critical event which turned the Pai to widespread warfare appears to have been the murder of one of their major leaders, Wauba Yuma. In October of 1866 the Superintendent of Indian Affairs for the Arizona Territory reported:

"They have been considered as in a state of war with the whites for more than a year past. An attempt was made last spring through Triteba, the head chief of the Mojaves, to arrange a peace . . . but the unprovoked murder of one of their influential chiefs by a party of whites resulted in the breaking off of all negotiations and a renewal of the war" (U. S. Senate 1936: 40, George W. Leihy report).

The following year the agent for the Colorado River Indians reported that: "The conduct of the Hualapais the past year has been very reprehensible . . . a fierce and vindictive band . . . are determined to avail themselves of every favorable opportunity to make war on the friendly Mohaves and the whites" (John Feudge in U. S. Senate 1936: 41).

Beginning in the summer of 1867, the U. S. Army began a forceful campaign against the Pai that by the fall of the following year had driven the Indians to sue for peace. The sub-district commander reported that on August 19, 1868, "As I was leaving this Post I was informed that a party of Hualapais were in the valley and desired to have a talk. The next day, Hleva-Hleva, the principal Captain of the Hualapais South of the Mojave Road, with about thirty Indians, came into this camp. He said the Hualapais desired peace . . ." (Lt. Col. William R. Price to Col. John P. Sherbourne in U. S. Senate 1936: 72).

With the progress of the fighting, the Army defined itself in Pai minds as a greater threat than the settlers. Punished by a superior force, they capitulated. In 1869, "on Jany. 1st, Lleva Lleva, the peaceful Chief of the Hualapais Indians, came into the Post with a few Indians and said that he and his band did not want to fight, and said that they were willing to do anything I wanted so that they should not be killed" (Price to Sherbourne in U. S. Senate 1936: 64).

The Pai had not succeeded in removing the cause of the original stress. Anglo-American settlements were re-established in their ancestral territory with the enforced peace. So in the decade following 1869 they were involved in a situation of great confusion. In the fall of 1871, as Anglo settlement and mining re-opened, they were given a helping hand of sorts by their conquerors. An Indian Bureau official appealed to the commander of the Department of Arizona: "As there are a number of Hualapais Indians reported to be in a destitute condition in the neighborhood of Beal Spring Camp, Arizona Territory, who have lately been peaceable, will you have the kindness to see that they are fed, protected, and otherwise cared for . . .?" (Vincent Colyer to Maj. Gen. George Crook in U. S. Senate 1936: 93).

By that time there was apparently a good deal of apathy in Pai reactions to situations wherein stresses of various kinds exceeded their tolerance thresholds. The next capricious action of the Anglo authorities arose from desires of officials of the Indian Bureau and the Army rather than from any overt Pai action.

"At that time . . . they all got together at Beale Springs. They were kind of scared. Looked like something [was] going to happen to them.

[51]

Anyhow, they were there for some time. During that time, the army officers gave them some flour, some things to eat, some meat, beef, while they were there at Beale Springs" (authors' field notes).

The Indian agent at the Colorado River Reservation had other plans for the Pai. He reported that: "It is my intention to remove them to this reservation in October next, where they can be fed with less expense to the government" (J. A. Tonner in U. S. Senate 1936: 96). As a Pai who witnessed the events put it: "The Government's man Dr. Tonner running the Indian Agency down at Parker said 'I like to have them Walapai Indians down here around Parker.'

"And he got to talking to General Crook. General Crook say it is all right. And this Doctor Tonner tell them people they're going to have the Walapai Indian down to Parker.

"The Walapai chiefs, all them chiefs: 'No, we ain't going to take that. That place is too hot. We don't want to go there.'

"And still this Indian Agent said: 'You got to take it.'

"All these Indians said, 'No, we ain't agoing to take it.' All Walapai Indians, we skipped off, going down into Grand Canyon get out of the way" (authors' field notes).

During this flight from the Beale Springs military reservation, the Pai turned to hunting cattle for sustenance. Having acquired a taste for beef from the rations issued them there, and lacking any real comprehension of Anglo-American attitudes toward property in cattle, they simply hunted the animals which had replaced the wild game on which they had formerly depended. There was probably an additional element of destructive action directed at the cattle as substitutes for their owners whom the Pai did not quite dare to attack directly. Afterwards, one large rancher tried to persuade the government to pay him "for three hundred and fifty six beef cattle, one hundred and six cows, and seven horses taken from him by the Hualapai Indians, and used by them for their subsistence while temporarily absent from their reservation between the first day of February, 1874, and the thirty-first day of March, 1874" (AA Feb. 4, 1882).

The army sent out troops in reprisal, but they were held up by floods, fortunately for the Pai, and "in the mean time, through the personal exertions of Captain Byrne, commanding Camp Beale's Springs, prompted also by fear of the troops, they all came in and agreed to go peaceable to the Colorado, which they did" (Gen. George Crook in U. S. Senate 1936: 97).

One year in the Colorado River bottomlands was all the Pai could endure as they watched relatives dying off rapidly. On April 20, 1875, they fled La Paz, where they were held, to return to their homes. "When we start to come back, up to the mountain . . . after passed *Ookwata Giyo'*, all them Indians rushing to come home . . . glad pretty close to the country, they just rush . . . run, come back as far as they make it to *Teki'aulva* and then they scattered. They go to their own place where they belong . . . Beale Springs, lot of peoples go to *Hel* (Milkweed Canyon), go Sandy, Wickiup, lot of peoples go to Fort Rock, Willows . . ." (authors' field notes).

The Pai had made their choice. They would pay any price in subordinate group status and social humiliation to remain in their ancestral homeland, even as beggars before their Anglo-American conquerors.

In-Group Aggression

By the time they returned to their own territory from the Colorado River Reservation, the Pai had learned that any overt hostility response to stress originating from contact with Anglos only resulted in their punishment in a very direct and physical form. Thereafter, their response when their tolerance-for-stress threshold was exceeded tended to take the form of marked in-group hostility and aggression as well as apathy. The Laboratory of Anthropology 1929 field party learned of at least two western band men who had "recently" committed suicide after killing their unfaithful spouses (Kroeber 1935: 141). This kind of aggression within the Pai population began many years earlier in the period after the flight from riverine captivity and before the advent of the ghost dance movement offered a brief emotional alternative. One recorded example occurred May 20, 1886, at Stockton Hill, a mining camp just north of Kingman in the Cerbat Mountains. In the words of a *Miner* correspondent . . .

> "Early this morning our quiet camp was aroused by the sound of several rifle shots at the Indian camp nearby. Half an hour later other shots were heard in quick succession, and excited Indians were seen running in every direction. It being about 6 a.m., when

[53]

most of the miners were on their way to work, about twenty of them went down to the Indian camp to investigate. On arriving at the camp they found a terrible state of affairs, two of the Indians having been killed and four others wounded. Those killed outright were a buck who went by the name of Ah Quinthe . . . and his squaw, who was a daughter of Chief Leve-Leve. Another buck, McCarty, was shot through the body, as was also another of Leve-Leve's daughters, a big squaw named Kate. Both of these are mortally wounded and will die in a few hours. Another squaw had received two balls in her leg, one of which had shattered the ankle bone . . .

"From what I can learn the trouble originated from jealousy, a squaw being the cause of it all. The Indian who did the killing went by the name of Pizzar, and has been in the employ of Sheriff Steen more or less of the time for the last three or four years . . . The whole tribe is gathering and more trouble will be up soon, as of course the Indians must have revenge . . . The murderer has fled, but is being pursued by three mounted Indians armed with Winchester rifles . . ." (MCM May 23, 1866).

On a lesser scale but likely more typical was the action of a Pai in 1888. "A Walapai Indian known as 'Bob' got drunk Wednesday and drove a knife into the head of a squaw known as 'Georgia,' making a dangerous and perhaps fatal wound. Bob was arrested by Sheriff Steen . . ." (MCM May 19, 1888). In this same general period, Lookup Dick reportedly shot himself to avoid being jailed for theft, according to a 1929 respondent (Kroeber 1935: 219). Drunken aggression seems from the newspaper record to have been the more common form of violence:

"At Mineral Park last Sunday a squaw stole considerable whiskey from a saloon and divided it up among the Indians. One of the number became insanely drunk and went over to the Indian camp at Canyon Station, where he found an old squaw and her buck, whom he beat unmercifully with rocks and clubs. The Indians came to town and reported the outrage to the sheriff" (MCM June 27, 1891).

Apprehended, the assailant was tried and sentenced to a thirty-day term in the Mohave County jail.

[54]

Under the stressful conditions of Pai contact with Anglo-Americans, infanticide directed at hybrid offspring appeared:

"There is a squaw now in jail who a few weeks ago murdered her pappoose at Hackberry . . . The details of the shocking crime have just come to light. It appears that the squaw gave birth to a halfbreed papoose and that another squaw suggested that it being no good it had better be killed. Another squaw, wishing to save the babe's life, carried it to the house of one of Hackberry's good citizens, where she was at work. In the evening she returned to camp and laid the babe beside the mother. The inhuman creature threw the little one from her and when it set up a piteous wail, she picked up a handful of sand and poured it into the child's mouth, and then taking a rock she beat it into insensibility. It was left on the cold ground all night and in the morning was cold and stiff in death . . ." (MCM Nov. 28, 1891).

Thus, all types of sources reveal the in-group and self-aggression current among the northeastern Pai in the 1880's and early 1890's in the face of Anglo-American domination, and the collective Pai decision that living in the ancestral homeland was worth whatever risk it entailed. That the risk was considerable is indicated in the newspaper files that recorded details about specific incidents of Pai homicide and suicide.

Aggression Release

The psychological climate indicated by occurrences such as those described above, and produced by the historical nature of Pai-Anglo-American contacts, was ideal for the introduction of a messianic movement with a nativistic dogma such as the ghost dance.

This movement was a logical development from native Pai religious beliefs and ceremonial patterns, plus a few additions learned from their conquerors. (It seems that the Pai, like other transculturating groups, could not distinguish always between truly Pai or Indian and Old World cultural elements). The ghost dance concepts were basically familiar, though couched in new terms and with new goals meaningful under the stresses of Anglo-American superordinance. The dance figures, the central pole, the trance visions were all known, so that they

[55]

offered an apparent opportunity to achieve millenial goals with familiar magical tools.

Significantly, the ghost dance offered to the Pai a form of physical release for their pent-up aggressions which they had not possessed before. This form of aggressive action did not, moreover, result in immediate and direct punishment by the settlers, although it came very close to doing so. This is certainly in accord with Linton's (1943: 231) statement that "the Ghost Dance laid great stress on the revival of such distinctive elements of Indian culture . . . which could be revived under agency conditions." The ghost dance ceremonial was a very efficient mechanism for the relief of stresses impinging on the Pai. One might assume that some such mystical response would have occurred in any event.

Only when the messianic doctrine of the ghost dance was put to the actual test of attempted resuscitation of a newly-deceased individual did the movement cease to function as a satisfactory aggression release for the Pai.

Chapter Six

POST-GHOST DANCE TRENDS

AFTER IT APPEARED that the ghost dance movement offered no real solution to the omnipresent sources of psychological stress, Pai responses to contact with Anglos tended to revert to an individual level until the missionaries seeking new converts to several evangelical Christian sects brought to them opportunities for belief in a different class of "millenary promises" (Mair 1959: 124), couched in terms of general salvation of Indians and other races alike.

Thus, further religious change laid at least some of the social foundations for bridging the wide conceptual gap that at first existed between the Pai and their Anglo-American conquerors. Christianity offered the prospect of a perfect world in which both living and dead would reunite without the ills of worldly travail even more than did the ghost dance movement. Christianity was taught in the Indian Bureau schools (Iliff 1954: 26, 69) which were started on the foundations laid by the Indian Association of Massachusetts, which sent the first missionary teacher to the western Pai bands in the mid 1890's (MCM May 26, 1894; U. S. Senate 1936: 176). She opened a school at Hackberry. A teacher for a new Indian day school in Kingman arrived late in October of 1896 (MCM Oct. 24, 1896) and the school opened early in November (MCM Nov. 7, 1896) with an enrollment of thirty to forty pupils (U. S. Senate 1936: 181). The pupils were almost immediately exposed to Christian instruction. On Christmas Day of 1896, "the Wallapai Indian school children received presents of candies, nuts, picture books, etc. Considerable clothing was also distributed amongst the aboriginees" (MCM Dec. 26, 1896). This gift distribution may well have been the first occasion when many northeastern Pai experienced Anglo-American generosity in a formal Christian context.

The Pai religious congregations established under missionary direction remain, however, under missionary leadership. So it was not until the Indian Reorganization Act of 1934 (48 Stat. 984) afforded the Pai an opportunity to build a new socio-political structure within which they could again act effectively on a group basis, that some measure of autonomy and self-fulfillment through group decision-making has returned to the Pai population.

This formal tribal organization is dual, a tribal council governing the Havasupai Reservation and another tribal council governing the Hualapai Reservation. Thus, the contact-period dominant group tendency to view the eastern and western bands of the northeastern Pai as different tribes has been sanctified by creating reservation governments responsive to 20th Century conditions rather than reflective of aboriginal northeastern Pai unity.

The ghost dance movement introduced among the Pai in 1889 proved to be the opening wedge in effectively splitting asunder the aboriginal polity.

Acknowledgments

THIS STUDY is based largely on material collected while the authors were engaged in research for the Hualapai and Havasupai tribes of Arizona and their general counsel, Royal D. Marks. The staff of the Arizona Pioneers' Historical Society was unfailingly helpful in the search for printed information. Dr. Cara E. Richards helped to locate and transcribe pertinent articles. Many of the photographs included herein are reproduced with the kind permission of the Southwest Museum, Los Angeles. We owe many thanks to numerous Hualapai and Havasupai with whom we discussed the ghost dance movement. Permission to quote from copyrighted sources has been given for the following:

Parsons, Elsie Clews (ed.) *Hopi Journal of Alexander M. Stephen.* New York: Columbia University Press, 1936.

Spicer, Edward H. *Cycles of Conquest.* Tucson: University of Arizona Press, 1962.

Miller, Joseph (compiler and ed.) *The Arizona Story.* New York: Hastings House, 1952.

Finally, we owe a debt of gratitude to Elizabeth Euler, William Hoyt, and Lucille Preston who assisted materially in the preparation of this manuscript for final publication.

References

ABERLE, DAVID F.
1959   "The Prophet Dance and Reactions to White Contact," *Southwestern Journal of Anthropology*, 15:1 (Spring) 74-83.

AA (*Alta Arizona*)
Established 1881, Mineral Park, Mohave County, Arizona Territory; a weekly.

AC (*Arizona Champion*)
Flagstaff, Coconino County, Arizona Territory.

ANONYMOUS
1892   "Ghost Dance in Arizona," *Journal of American Folklore*, 5:16.

ANONYMOUS
1899   "The Yava-Supai Indian," *The Arizona Graphic*, Vol. 14, Oct. 7.

AWJ (*Arizona Weekly Journal*)
Prescott, Yavapai County, Arizona Territory.

BIEBER, RALPH P. (editor)
1939   "Diaries of Francois Xavier Aubry, 1853-1854," *Exploring Southwestern Trails, 1846-1854*. Glendale: Arthur H. Clark Co.

BISHOP, T. A.
1885   Letter to Office of Indians Affairs, National Archives, OIA, Letters Received, 1885, E-17391.

BOURKE, JOHN G.
1891   *On the Border With Crook*. New York: Charles Scribners Sons.

BRAYTON, LT. COL. E. M.
1888   Telegram to Adjutant General, Dept. of Arizona, Los Angeles, Calif. National Archives, Records of the Bureau of Indian Affairs, Letters Received, 4739-1888.

COUES, ELLIOT
1900   *On the Trail of a Spanish Pioneer*. New York: Harpers.

DAVIS, A. E.
1882   "The Wallapais," *Alta Arizona*, I: 31 (May 13).

DOBYNS, HENRY F. AND ROBERT C. EULER
1960   "A Brief History of the Northeastern Pai," *Plateau*, 32:3.

DUBOIS, CORA
1939   *The 1870 Ghost Dance*. Anthropological Records 3:1; Berkeley: University of California Press.

ERASMUS, CHARLES J.
1961   *Man Takes Control*. Minneapolis: University of Minnesota Press.

EULER, ROBERT C.
1966a   "Ethnographic Methodology: A Tri-Chronic Study in Culture Change,

Informant Reliability and Validity from the Southern Paiute," *American Historical Anthropology. Essays in Honor of Leslie Spier.* Carbondale: Southern Illinois University Press (in press).

1966b *Southern Paiute Ethnohistory.* Salt Lake City: University of Utah Anthropological Papers No. 78.

GAYTON, A. H.

1930 *The Ghost Dance of 1870 in South-Central California.* University of California Publications in American Archaeology and Ethnology 23:3.

HARRIS, JACK S.

1940 "The White Knife Shoshone of Nevada," *Acculturation in Seven American Indian Tribes*, Ralph Linton, editor. New York: D. Appleton-Century Co.

ILIFF, FLORA GREGG

1954 *People of the Blue Water.* New York: Harpers.

INDIAN CLAIMS COMMISSION

1950 *In the Matter of the Perpetuation of Testimony of Aged Members of the Hualapai Tribe of Indians.* Aug. 5, 1950 (typescript).

JAMES, GEORGE WHARTON

1903 *The Indians of the Painted Desert Region.* Boston: Little, Brown & Co.

KROEBER, A. L. (editor)

1935 *Walapai Ethnography.* Menasha, Wisc: American Anthropological Association Memoir No. 42.

LEIGHTON, ALEXANDER H.

1949 *Human Relations in a Changing World.* New York: E. P. Dutton & Co.

LINTON, RALPH

1943 "Nativistic Movements," *American Anthropologist*, 45:2.

MAIR, L. P.

1959 "Independent Religious Movements in Three Continents," *Comparative Studies in Society and History*, I:2 (January) 113-36.

McCOWAN, S. M.

1890 Letter to Office of Indian Affairs, National Archives, OIA, Letters Received, 1890, E-28941.

MEAD, MARGARET

1959 "Independent Religious Movements," *Comparative Studies in Society and History*, I:4 (June) 324-9.

MERTON, ROBERT K.

1957 *Social Theory and Social Structure.* Glencoe, Ill: Free Press (revised edition).

MILLER, JOSEPH (compiler and editor)

1952 *The Arizona Story.* New York: Hastings House.

MCM (*Mohave County Miner*)

Established 1892, a weekly. (First published at Mineral Park, Arizona

Territory, 1882-7; moved to Kingman, A. T., January, 1887).

MOONEY, JAMES
    1896 *The Ghost Dance Religion and the Sioux Outbreak of 1890.* Washington: Bureau of American Ethnology, 14th Annual Report (1892-1893), Part 2.

MURDOCK, GEORGE P.
    1959 *Africa: Its Peoples and Their Culture History.* New York: McGraw-Hill.
    1963 "Ethnographic Atlas," *Ethnology 2:4.*

NASH, PHILLEO
    1955 "The Place of Religious Revivalism in the Formation of the Intercultural Community on Klamath Reservation," *Social Anthropology of the North American Tribes,* (Fred Eggan, editor), Chicago: University of Chicago Press.

PARSONS, ELSIE CLEWS
    1936 *Hopi Journal of Alexander M. Stephen.* New York: Columbia University Press.

SPICER, EDWARD H.
    1962 *Cycles of Conquest.* Tucson: University of Arizona Press.

SPIER, LESLIE
    1928 *Havasupai Ethnography.* American Museum of Natural History, Anthropological Papers, 29:3.

UDELL, JOHN
    1866 *Journal of John Udell, Kept During a Trip Across the Plains, Containing an Account of the Massacre of a Portion of His Party by the Mohave Indians in 1859.* Jefferson: Ashtabula Sentinel Steam Press (Los Angeles: N. A. Kovach reprint, 1946).

U. S. SENATE
    1936 *Walapai Papers.* Senate document No. 273, 74th Congress, 2nd Session, Washington, D. C.

VOGET, FRED
    1948 "Individual Motivation in the Diffusion of the Wind River Shoshone Sundance to the Crow Indians," *American Anthropologist,* 50:4.

WALLACE, ANTHONY F. C.
    1956 "Revitalization Movements," *American Anthropologist,* 58:2 (April) 264-281.

Index

The Ghost Dance of 1889
has been set in Linotype Caledonia
and printed on Beckett Laid Text by
Northland Press, Flagstaff, Arizona. It
was designed by Paul Weaver

"This book empowers kids with practical, fun strategies for challenges like waking up, making friends, keeping calm, paying attention, and handling situations like lunch and recess. It also empowers parents with tools to help kids get ready in the morning, handle homework, and more. A supercharged, super powerful book!"

—*Lindsey Biel, M.A., OTR/L, Occupational Therapist,*
Author of Sensory Processing Challenges: Effective Clinical
Work with Kids & Teens, *www.sensorysmarts.com*

"Practical methods that children can easily understand and use."

—*Dr. Temple Grandin, author of*
Thinking in Pictures *and* The Autistic Brain

"Lauren Brukner has penned a fun and practical guide for kids and parents alike to develop Self-Control Super-Powers! *Self-Control to the Rescue* is certain to help kids have fewer tough times, and more of the success and happiness that are rights of childhood."

—*Alex Doman, founder and CEO Advanced Brain Technologies,*
bestselling co-author Healing at the Speed of Sound

"When we are helping children to manage upset feelings, our strategies must be practical, flexible, and appealing. In *Self-Control to the Rescue!*, Lauren Brukner's fourth book, she once again delivers child-friendly learning activities, great illustrations and authoritative advice in a package that children will certainly enjoy and parents and professionals will find immediately applicable."

—*Joel Shaul, licensed clinical social worker and*
author of The Green Zone Conversation Book

"Here at last is a book for parents and therapists to use with children to help them develop self-regulation! Lauren Brukner enchants us with a fun-filled but deep approach that allows us to take a closer activity-oriented look at our interactions with children who have regulation challenges. Reading her evocative ideas will help every parent, teacher, and child to approach self-regulation from a supportive, fun direction, and will transform your activities with children from stressful to playful. This book is for people everywhere who want to create a regulated place within themselves and the children with whom they live or love."

—*Lucy Jane Miller, Ph.D, OTR, founder of STAR Institute for SPD by the same author*

**Stay Cool and In Control
with the Keep-Calm Guru**
**Wise Ways for Children to
Regulate their Emotions and Senses**
Lauren Brukner
Illustrated by Apsley
ISBN 978 1 78592 714 0
eISBN 978 1 78450 300 0

**How to Be a Superhero
Called Self-Control!**
**Super Powers to Help Younger Children
to Regulate their Emotions and Senses**
Lauren Brukner
Illustrated by Apsley
ISBN 978 1 84905 717 2
eISBN 978 1 78450 203 4

**The Kids' Guide to Staying
Awesome and In Control**
**Simple Stuff to Help Children
Regulate their Emotions and Senses**
Lauren Brukner
Illustrated by Apsley
ISBN 978 1 84905 997 8
eISBN 978 0 85700 962 3

of related interest

Seahorse's Magical Sun Sequences
**How all children (and sea creatures) can use yoga
to feel positive, confident and completely included**
Michael Chissick
Illustrated by Sarah Peacock
ISBN 978 1 84819 283 6
eISBN 978 0 85701 230 2

Sitting on a Chicken
The Best (Ever) 52 Yoga Games to Teach in Schools
Michael Chissick
Illustrated by Sarah Peacock
ISBN 978 1 84819 325 3
eISBN 978 0 85701 280 7

Starving the Anxiety Gremlin
**A Cognitive Behavioural Therapy Workbook
on Anxiety Management for Young People**
Kate Collins-Donnelly
ISBN 978 1 84905 341 9
eISBN 978 0 85700 673 8

SELF-CONTROL
TO THE RESCUE!

Super-Powers to Help Kids Through
the Tough Stuff in Everyday Life

LAUREN BRUKNER
ILLUSTRATED BY APSLEY

Jessica Kingsley *Publishers*
London and Philadelphia

This book, and all of the strategies provided, are not intended to provide medical or diagnostic information. This book is not a replacement for occupational therapy, physical therapy, vision therapy, speech therapy, or any other specific services your child may need. If your child has a suspected or diagnosed medical condition, speak with your paediatrician before engaging in any suggested exercises, or trying any tools or strategies, to ensure that they are safe and appropriate.

First published in 2017
by Jessica Kingsley Publishers
73 Collier Street
London N1 9BE, UK
and
400 Market Street, Suite 400
Philadelphia, PA 19106, USA

www.jkp.com

Library of Congress Cataloging in Publication Data
A CIP catalog record for this book is available from the Library of Congress

British Library Cataloguing in Publication Data
A CIP catalogue record for this book is available from the British Library

ISBN 978 1 78592 759 1
eISBN 978 1 78450 619 3

Printed and bound in the United States

To the educators and therapists, who give
their time, patience, energy, and love.

To the parents, who give their very soul.

Last, to the children themselves, who deserve
all of this, and appreciate it more than
we can ever know in our lifetimes.

Acknowledgements

As I finish up the last page of this manuscript, I find myself, yet again, thanking my wonderfully patient, amazing, and brilliant commissioning editor, Rachel Menzies. Her willingness to go to bat for the message in all the books in this series, patience in the process, endless editing hours, back-and-forth emails overseas, and true belief in the vision of this book, and hopeful impact on the lives of families and educators, has helped to develop it from an idea spoken about through email to the actual book that you are holding in your hands and reading at this very moment. Rachel—you are a true rock star, and so very appreciated.

Thank you, yet again, to the fantastic editorial, production, and marketing teams at Jessica Kingsley Publishers—I often wake up in the morning feeling so blessed to write for a publishing company that values the benefit of publishing books that make a difference in the lives of others. I am beyond thankful that I am afforded with the opportunity to write books that can positively touch the lives of others.

To my husband: I can never put my love for you into words here, so I'm not going to start now. I love you and appreciate you always, always. You are my everything.

To my children: I hope that as you see me pushing myself to accomplish my dreams of being an author while working full time and always, always, your mom first (and it's not always easy to balance it all), know first and foremost that you are my number one. As long as you put your heart, soul, and body into your dreams, and you know with everything that you've got that you've tried your best, you will move mountains, kids.

Contents

PART 1

FOR KIDS

Introduction

The real super-powers of self-control

Well, hello, awesome and amazing readers. That's right, I'm talking to you! The one with the eyes looking into this book, or the ears hearing the words being read. Clap three times to show me how excited you are to start this adventure!

By now, I'm sure you've heard of me. Da da da da—Self-Control, super-hero extraordinaire, to the rescue! What? You haven't? Are you sure? I bet you have. I'll tell you why.

Have you ever gotten so, so angry, that you just felt like you wanted to explode with the force of it—but you didn't? Well, that was the super-powers of Self-Control, channeling the force to you.

What about feeling so, so wiggly, so unfocused, that you were unable to listen to your teacher in class, but you somehow got the willpower to bring your body and mind back to your lesson? Again, that's the super-powers of Self-Control to the rescue!

I could keep going, but I think that you're starting to get the idea.

I may not be as glamorous, as "pretty," or as, well, green, as some of my more famous super-hero buddies, but I think that my own super-hero powers are pretty important, don't you? Plus, don't tell them I told you, but I have helped them out quite a bit to get them where they are today.

Are you ready to learn some Self-Control Super-Powers? Let's go!

How this book works

It's officially time to begin your training. Put on your capes and let's enter Self-Control Academy! Open the door, it's kind of heavy—you may need both hands!

Ok, guys. We're going to learn super-powers while helping fellow kids who are facing trouble:

- sleeping

- waking up

- paying attention

- with friends

- at recess and lunch.

When you do the strategy the right way—trust me, I'm watching—you save the day for that kid.

I know they will thank you for it.

You will also earn a Self-Control Coin.

Once you earn all 15 coins, you graduate and are an official Self-Control Super-Hero—able to rescue kids from tough situations that we will practice (with your grown-up's permission, of course).

Push your hands together, and let's dive into the book. Self-Controls to the rescue!

CHAPTER 1

Getting Ready in the Morning

"Waking up is hard to do..." I think that's part of a song. For good reason. Warm, cozy bed. Facing the day. Ugh! I get it.

So, so many people, kids and adults alike, have a lot of trouble even getting out of their beds, let alone being on time doing everything else so that they can get to school and work on time. It can be very stressful, can't it?

This chapter is going to give you three simple ways to make the first part, just getting out of bed, a bit easier, so that the rest of the morning can go smoother. Happier you—happier family.

Let's practice by helping Joel, Lianna, and Charlie. Before we begin, do you have trouble with waking up in the morning? If you're reading this with a friend or in a group, touch your left knee if you would like to share what feels difficult or your own ways that help you get yourself out of bed!

Super-Power #1: Picture Your Day Going Great!

Joel is curled up under the soft blankets of his bed. The clock reads 7:50 a.m., and school starts at 8:00 a.m. His sisters have already dressed and eaten breakfast. He hears them laughing downstairs, which just makes him feel irritated. Joel has been having a hard time in school lately, especially with understanding math. The thought of going into class makes him feel nervous. He can't find the words to say this to his dad, so he simply states angrily: "I am not going to school now! It's just going to be bad. I want to stay at home." His dad throws his hands up, and walks out of the room.

Ok, guys, here is our first assignment. We have to help Joel feel better about himself, while getting him out of bed. This is a complicated case for our first job, but I know that you can do it!

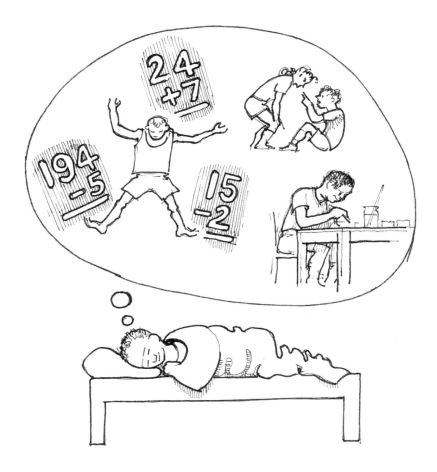

The first super-power is called **Picture Your Day Going Great!** Close your eyes. Now, in your mind, go through the day. What do you anticipate happening—great things, ok things, and maybe more difficult things? Remind yourself there are things that may happen that you can't anticipate. Remind yourself that you can't control every situation, but you can control how you think about it, and your reaction. Picture yourself happy, flexible, and confident.

Let's see if we helped Joel! I hope so, don't you? It's so important to feel confident and happy in yourself.

Amazing job! Clap your hands nice and loud to make the first coin appear!

Super-Power #2: Reach Up and Grab the Sunshine to Your Heart!

The house is bustling with the sounds of the morning rush to get ready. "It's cold outside, make sure you put your scarf by your backpack!" "Do you want waffles with melon or with an apple?" Lianna is still in bed. Her sister is dressed, and fixing her hair in the room that they share. Lianna, flopped sideways across her bed, hair disheveled, rubs her eyes and mutters angrily, "It's too bright in here! I want to sleep!"

I've felt that way before, haven't you? Snap twice and touch your nose so I know you're ready for action! For the first super-power, we didn't need to open our eyes (or move), right? This next one requires a bit more work, but Lianna (or you!) can still lay down.

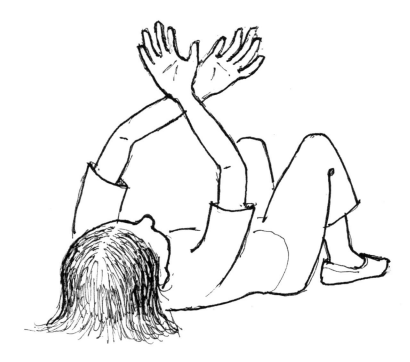

Super-Power #2 is called **Reach Up and Grab the Sunshine to Your Heart!** This works, even if it's a cloudy day, because the sun always peeks out through the clouds, if you just search for it. What you're going to do is reach up, from either laying down or seated, cross your arms across each other, and stretch your arms upwards towards the sunshine. Take some of that sunshine and put it to your heart. Press it there as long as it takes to stick. Let this sunshine start your day brightly. Touch that place in your heart whenever you need, throughout the day, to remind yourself of that brightness, and that everything is, or will be, ok.

Ok, back to Lianna. Let's see if using this new super-power, **Reach Up and Grab the Sunshine to Your Heart!**, helped Lianna wake up happy and easily.

Fantastic! Snap your fingers to make your 2 coins appear!

Super-Power #3: Brisk Rub to Get Moving!

Charlie didn't sleep the night before. He kept tossing and turning. The room was too hot. Then the room was too cold. He had strange dreams. When his mom woke him up in the morning, his whole body felt like lead. "I can't move!" His mom takes off the covers. Still he doesn't budge. Now Charlie's mom is getting upset. "It's school in 15 minutes. I let you oversleep, and now I'm going to be late for work!"

The dreaded Night-With-No-Sleep. It happens to the best of us. Sometimes, no matter how much you try, it can be super-hard to fall asleep. Whether there is a lot on your mind, you're feeling sick, you have a ton of energy…well, Chapter 5, later on, focuses on ways to reduce how many times those nights happen. Good news, huh? I know, that was one of the most exciting parts of this book for me, too!

Anyway, for now, let's help Charlie. We can't give him back his night of sleep. He has to get to school. Let's make it easier for him to get out of bed, right? Are you ready? Wiggle your fingers four times, and blink twice to show me you're pumped. Ok!

Super-Power #3 is called **Brisk Rub to Get Moving!** This can be done from a seated or standing position. Cross your arms, open your palms, and quickly rub your arms, legs, the tops of your hands, and feet, up and down.

Amazing! Let's check in with Charlie later in his day. I hope this made a difference, and he is doing ok!

You rock! Wiggle your shoulders to make all 3 coins appear!

CHAPTER 2

Paying Attention

How many times have you heard *"Pay attention!"* in your life? I can't count how many times I've heard it before in mine! You know, when I was a kid, before I became a super-hero as a full-time job, I went to school, just like you. When stuff I was being taught felt hard for me, sometimes my mind automatically turned off because I JUST DIDN'T GET IT. Other times, I did it on purpose, because when I didn't understand things, I got scared or embarrassed, and thought, "What's the point of listening? I'm just getting more and more confused!" Honestly, I was also a super-wiggly kid. Back in those days, teachers didn't get it the way they do now. I just had to sit and sit and my mind would almost turn off like a light. I want to ask you to be super-honest here. Can you relate to anything I just shared?

What I want you to do is show a thumbs-up if you have trouble paying attention when you don't understand what you're learning—and your mind wanders.

Please touch your right elbow if you have trouble paying attention because you get scared or embarrassed when you don't understand what you're learning (or another similar feeling about something else that you find difficult).

Finally, rub your ears if you have trouble paying attention because your body needs to move and you feel like you sit for too long.

Wow, you guys are awesome and super-brave. Thank you for sharing with me.

This chapter is going to give you three simple ways to make paying attention a bit easier. Let's practice by helping Isaiah, Joey, and Ron.

Super-Power #4: Thought Box

Isaiah is working hard on his math. He can't help but think about a playdate that is happening in the afternoon. He runs it over and over in his head. Pictures and images of what may happen at the playdate keep running through his mind: the slide, the park, board games, eating snacks side by side, and laughing. He runs to tell his teacher all about his playdate later. "We're not talking about that right now, Isaiah."

Have you ever been so excited, happy, or even upset about something that happened, or perhaps that will happen, that it feels impossible to focus on what you're supposed to be doing? It happens to all of us sometimes. That's where Super-Power #4, **Thought Box**, comes in! Let's try it out and help Isaiah focus on his work proudly and do his best! Are you ready to try it out? Press your palms together to show me that you're ready!

Close your eyes. Picture in your mind a special box where you're going to place all of your distracting thoughts. What color is your box? Maybe it's more than one color! Is it smooth, or rough? Is it sparkly, plain, mesh? Does it have a pattern, shapes, designs? Does it have a lock, or does it stay closed on its own? If it has a lock, what does it look like? What does it feel like? Once you have it decorated (or not) in your mind, put all of those distracting thoughts inside the box. Close the lid tightly! If it has a lock, make sure to lock it! Now, you can open the box and come back to those distracting thoughts at another time when it's ok to think about them (like free time at your house, walking home from school, etc.).

Fantastic job! Let's see if the power of our Thought Box super-power was enough to help our Isaiah!

You did it! Now, reach up to the ceiling and touch the ground to make all 4 coins appear!

Super-Power #5: Squeeze Your Whole Body!

It's been a long day at school. Reading, writing, math, science, social studies. More writing. Sitting. Recess and lunch. More sitting and listening to the teacher. A long bus ride. Joey drags himself into the house, and tiredly hangs his coat and backpack on the hook in the entryway. "Homework?!" he thinks to himself. He tries his best to sit and do all his work. Somehow, he just can't do it! It just feels so much better to just hang upside down from the couch! His whole body relaxes. "What are you doing?" his mom asks sternly. "Go back and do your homework!" "But I can't!" he yells. "You can, and you will!" she exclaims, as she begins dinner.

I understand how Joey feels. Can you? Give yourself a tight hug and count to ten by twos if you can relate. School can feel long and overwhelming, a place where you sometimes really try your best as much as possible, no? And then you get home. And. There's. More. Work. Ugh! Well, as we said before, we can't change other people or other situations, that's not one of my super-powers, but we can change our reactions—that *is* one thing!

Let's help Joey with Super-Power #5, **Squeeze Your Whole Body!** Close your eyes. Where do you feel your wiggles the most? In your belly? Your feet? Your arms, legs, fingers, head? A mixture? Now, squeeze your entire body—tight, tight, tight, like you're making a huge muscle out of your whole body—and feel the wiggles squeeze out of it. Ahh, doesn't that feel better?

Let's check in on Joey. Do you think he moved past the couch? I hope so, or it's going to be such a long night for the poor kid.

I'm so proud of you! Now, blink twice, and touch your ears to make all 5 coins appear.

Super-Power #6: Squeeze into a Ball

The class is learning about subtraction. Ron is having difficulty understanding what the teacher is teaching. He's embarrassed to ask her to explain it in a different way, so, instead, he looks out the window. It's a beautiful day outside. He thinks about what he'll do when he gets home. Maybe he'll get to go to the park. Maybe he'll have pizza for dinner! Hopefully, his mom won't try to force him to eat asparagus again. He forgets where he is and what he is doing. Suddenly, all the kids are getting up from the rug and getting cubes, pencils, and workbooks. "Oh no," he thinks. "What are we doing? I have no idea how to do this."

It can be hard to pay attention when you don't understand what's being taught, and it can be even harder to ask for help when you need it. Do you agree? Tap your right knee three times if you do.

Let's learn Super-Power #6, **Squeeze into a Ball**, to help Ron feel more calm and focused, so that he can be less nervous when he needs to ask for help and ready to pay attention when he understands the lesson.

When you sit for a long time, it can be hard to feel where your body is. This can even make kids (and adults) feel nervous and upset! While sitting on the floor or in a chair, plant your feet to the floor or the seat of the chair, and squeeze your knees to your belly with your arms. Hold for 5–10 seconds.

Great! Let's see how Ron is doing. I hope we helped him build his confidence, along with his focus!

You did it again! Fantastic! Now, push the insides of your feet together—push, push, push! That will make all 6 coins appear.

CHAPTER 3

Recess and Lunch

Oh, the famous recess and lunch. Do you know how many times my Self-Control Beeper has gone off where teachers, principals, and kids have needed my help around the world? It's probably the most difficult part of the school day.

Why? You may be able to guess. Noisy, too many things to look at, maybe too little time to play before having to sit and learn again. The list goes on and on.

This chapter is going to give you three simple ways to help you not only get through, but enjoy it too, while also allowing the rest of the day to go more smoothly. Happier you, happier teacher, happier class!

Let's practice by helping Alex, Julie, and Evan. Before we begin, do you have trouble with enjoying recess and lunch, and then having an ok day afterwards? If you're reading this with a friend or in a group, cross your arms and tap your shoulders if you would like to share what feels difficult or your own ways that help you!

Super-Power #7: Take Space Inside Your Mind

The playground is super-crowded. Alex has been playing on the monkey bars happily for the past few minutes. The whistle sounds, and she lines up with her class. One boy begins yelling on the line. Noise makes her body feel scared. When she feels scared, it doesn't look like she's afraid, because she will usually act silly with her body and roll on the floor, laughing. This time, she screams back and moves her body very quickly, waving her lunch box back and forth. The recess teacher comes by, leading both Alex and the boy to take a break, a stern expression on her face.

Poor Alex! It's not her fault! We have to teach her a way to feel peaceful, even when her surroundings are, well, not. It's so important to think about what we can do in these kinds of situations. We can't change how loud the playground is, or how many people are close to us, but we can control our feelings. That's an awesome thought, isn't it?

One way to do that is through Super-Power #7, **Take Space Inside Your Mind**. This can be done without physically taking space, without moving a muscle. Are you ready? Wiggle your toes to show that you are! Breathe in, and out, slowly. Think of a place that makes you feel calm and peaceful. Picture every detail, what it looks like, what different objects there feel like, any smells, things that you hear. Picture yourself there. Where are you in that special place? What are you doing? When you're ready, open your eyes and join the group.

Let's check on Alex and see how she is doing. I hope that the strength of the **Take Space Inside Your Mind** super-power was enough to help her feel less afraid and have a nice afternoon!

You did it again! These kids are sure lucky to have you. Now, rub your hands together until they're nice and warm and cover your eyes for five seconds. Now, put your hands down. Let's see if all 7 coins appeared!

Super-Power #8: Focus on One Detail

It's pouring buckets outside. The class gives a collective groan as the teacher announces that it will have to be indoor recess. The recess teacher sets up tables, and assigns children to different stations. Every noise feels extra loud; every kid feels extra close as classmates try to let out extra energy in the confines of the classroom. Julie feels like she wants to shrink into herself. She moves from table to table, but everybody is too loud, too close. There is nowhere in the classroom to go to take space and have quiet, like her teacher and occupational therapist have taught her. She feels trapped!

Don't worry Julie—we are here to save the day! This new strategy is super-simple. I happen to use it when I get overwhelmed. Yes, just because I'm a super-hero doesn't mean I'm not human!

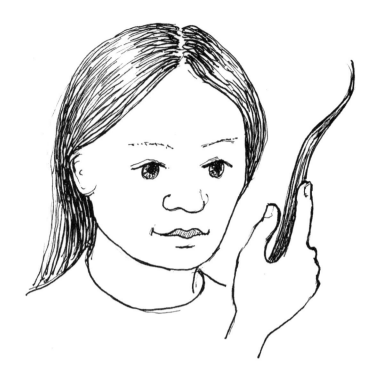

Bring each finger to your thumb on your right hand. Amazing! Let's learn Super-Power #8, **Focus on One Detail**. Look around. Find a point to focus on that makes you feel calmer. It can be a leaf, a pillow, a mark on the wall, a curve of the floor, even a blade of grass. Notice every detail about it. Block out the rest of the world. All that matters in this moment is that focus point. When you're ready, rejoin the group.

Let's check in on Julie. I hope that our hard work helped her feel not only calm, but happy, and ready to participate in recess.

Air-high-five me! Now, touch your head, nose, and left foot. This will help all 8 coins appear.

Super-Power #9: Focus on Your Breathing

Recess is over. Evan's class goes, single file, through a narrow hallway into the cafeteria, laughter and screams echoing and bouncing off the walls. Each loud noise pierces his ears, but he forces himself to keep going. They enter the cafeteria, and Evan squints under the harsh lighting. He finds a seat next to his friend, Michael. Kids are getting up from their seats, acting silly, laughing, arguing, and yelling as they scarf down lunch. Evan and Michael are quiet as they eat. A group of kids come and sit next to them, speaking loudly and making silly faces. Finally, Evan's had enough. He runs to the side of the cafeteria, and squeezes himself between two food carts, crying. Michael runs to tell the teacher, a worried expression on his face.

Poor guy! We have to help, and ASAP. A quick and effective way to calm down and feel less overwhelmed is to first gain control over our breathing, and then focus on it. That's where our next super-power comes in.

Reach and tap your left foot twice and your right foot three times if you're ready.

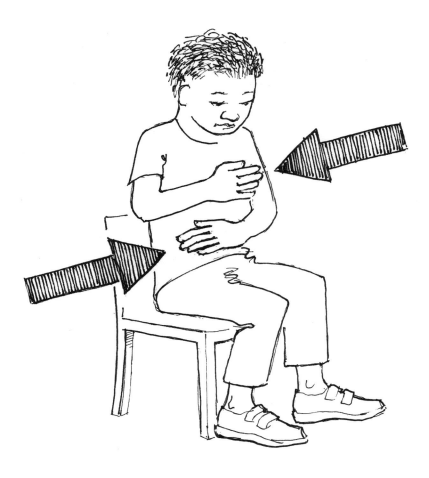

Super-Power #9 is called **Focus on Your Breathing**. Put one hand over your heart, and one hand over your belly. Breathe in slowly for three seconds, and breathe out for five seconds. Good. Now, focus all of your attention on how your breath is going in through your nose, and out of your mouth. Focus on how your hands rise on your chest as you breathe in, and fall on your chest as you breathe out. Focus on how your hands fall on your belly as you breathe in, and rise on your belly as you breathe out.

Now back to Evan. Let's see if our **Focus on Your Breathing** super-power helped him feel safe and calm.

Say it after me: "Oh yeah!" Your turn:_____. "We did it!" Your turn:_____. Great! Now, squeeze your hands together tightly for all 9 coins to appear!

CHAPTER 4

Friendship Tips

Friendship can be one of the most amazing parts of life; it can also be pretty difficult to manage. Tricky emotions definitely pop up, like anger, jealousy, frustration, and sadness. Happily, those feelings usually resolve and are often balanced by positive emotions such as happiness, silliness, excitement, and love. Arguments and disagreements are a natural part of friendships, and when handled appropriately, they can help each person learn about the other.

This chapter is going to give you three simple ways to help you work out disagreements, and some ways to compromise when spending time with friends. Let's practice by helping Camille, Ali, and Stephanie.

Before we begin, do you have trouble getting along with friends, or working out disagreements when they come up? If you're reading this with a friend or in a group, touch your fingertips together to show that you would like to share what feels difficult or your own ways that help you!

Super-Power #10: "Let's Take Turns Choosing What to Do"

"I don't want to do that." Camille sits with her arms crossed, as her friend offers game after game, activity after activity. "I just want to play tag." "But that's the one thing that I really don't want to play, Camille," her friend begs. "Isn't there any other game that you'll play with me? I'm the guest, anyway." Camille stomps up to her room, leaving her friend alone in the living room.

Uh oh. Have you ever been told, "You need to be flexible?" I have a super-hero friend who is so flexible that she can bend into an actual ball! Ok, off topic…

Anyway, it's important to think about both sides, both people in a friendship, and think about the other person. Sometimes, this is not an automatic thought. That's where this super-power comes in to help us, Super-Power #10, **"Let's Take Turns Choosing What to Do."** At the beginning of playing with a friend, whether it's at school or at home, start off right away saying: "Let's take turns choosing what to do." It's ok if you don't feel like doing this—even if you feel like doing the opposite (maybe you have a super-awesome game that you want to play the whole time!). This will start off the play with your friend in a kind and fair way, and will make playing with friends a whole lot easier. It will show that you're a kind and considerate friend who is also flexible. Repeating this throughout a playdate/play at school will prevent arguments and allow for everyone to get along!

How do you think Camille is doing? Maybe she became more flexible and is now able to play something with her friend that they both compromised on!

Do you feel yourselves turning into Self-Control Super-Heroes yet? I see it, even through the pages! Yep, you're doing that good a job. Blink your eyes and then rub your ears, so that 10 coins will appear.

Super-Power #11: "Let's Take Space for Five Minutes"

Ali and her friends are at recess. They're building a fort out of big foam blocks. An argument develops. "No, Ali, you took my block!" one of her friends says, grabbing the top piece. "That's so mean! Ask first!" Ali counters, and grabs it back. This goes on for a few minutes and, somehow, the fort is knocked down entirely. Ali begins to tear up. "Why are you laughing because I'm upset? You're not my friend anymore! This wouldn't have happened if you just shared!"

Sometimes, in the heat of the moment, we do or say things that we may regret later on. That's where the next super-power—Super-Power #11, **"Let's Take Space for Five Minutes"**—comes in.

Are you ready, Ali? We're on our way! Clap twice and blink once to show you're at the ready, kids.

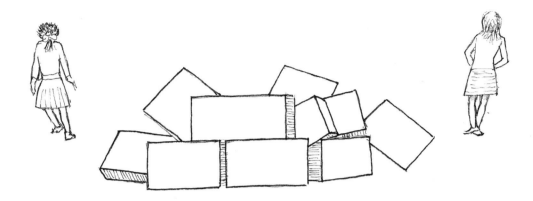

When you're having a difficult time expressing yourself to a friend, it's helpful to have an automatic saying, "Let's take space for five minutes," and walk away from the situation—even, and especially, when you don't feel like it. When you practice doing this automatically, it'll get you in the habit of taking space until you both have time to cool down and work it out in a calm way.

Let's check back in with Ali. Arguments happen. I bet their friendship is ok, especially with our hard work.

Doesn't it feel great to help kids become friends? It makes my heart feel that nice warm feeling. Wiggle the fingers on your left hand, then wiggle the fingers on your right hand, to make 11 coins appear.

Super-Power #12: Simple Steps to Solving Arguments

Stephanie woke up grumpy, even though it was a sunny Saturday morning. Her brother was getting on her nerves. Everything he said felt extra mean, extra bossy, or extra annoying. When she complained to her mom and dad, she got no sympathy. "You're the older one. You're not being kind. Make a change." It was the last straw when he grabbed the painting that she had just finished from the kitchen counter and his finger prints were all over the once-beautiful piece. She couldn't help it, she pushed him. "I hate you!" she cried, brushing away tears, running to her room. "Go work that out and make it right!" she hears her mom call from downstairs.

Siblings can make the best of friends. Those who love so much can fight so much, as well. Arguments between siblings can be pretty intense, am I right? Thumbs up if you can relate. When feelings get so strong, and you're told to work it out, it can be very helpful to have actual steps written down for you. That's where Super-Power #12, **Simple Steps to Solving Arguments**, comes in.

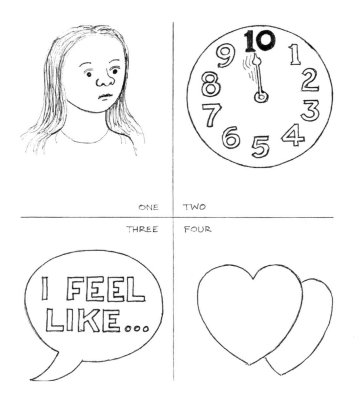

One/Two Take a deep breath or count to ten.

Three   Use your words to explain your feelings with an I Message ("I feel _____ because _____").

Four   Do something kind for each other.

Back to Stephanie. Let's see if the strength of the **Simple Steps to Solving Arguments Super-Power** helped her resolve her argument with her brother and make her day better. Sometimes, even doing an act of kindness for another person is enough to make you smile!

Woo-hoo! Give yourself a pat on the back for a job well done! Seriously. Tap yourself on the back five times (gently) to make all 12 coins appear.

CHAPTER 5

Bedtime

Bedtime. Another part of the day (well, night) where my Self-Control Beeper goes off almost constantly, with kids asking for help from all over the globe.

I get calls that kids don't want to go to bed, kids have trouble sleeping, that kids are waking up in the middle of the night—the list goes on and on. Thank goodness for 24-hour groceries. I get hungry in the middle of the night.

Anyway, there are so many reasons why kids have trouble sleeping. Sometimes, our minds feel like they're racing with thoughts and ideas. Other times, our minds may be filled with worries or fears. Our bodies may feel like they're filled with so much energy that when it's bedtime, it doesn't feel possible to slow down.

But here's the thing—our bodies *need* sleep. They're built to require a certain number of hours of sleep in order to stay healthy and happy.

This chapter is going to give you three simple ways to help you learn to fall asleep on your own—that's right, without a grown-up. Yes, you can do it! You're in Self-Control Academy, are you not?

Let's practice by helping Shayna, Flynn, and Max. Before we begin, do you have trouble with falling or staying asleep? If you're reading this with a friend or in a group, rub your hands together and cover your eyes to show that you would like to share what feels difficult or your own ways that help you!

Super-Power #13: The Journal in Your Mind

Shayna has been tossing and turning in her bed for what feels like hours. She can't stop thinking about what happened during school: friends, teachers, a difficult part of math. Her mind wanders to an upcoming holiday party. She wonders what family members will be there. Suddenly, she looks at the clock. It's been two hours since she went to bed! She yawns; she feels so tired, but just can't stop her thoughts from coming.

Sometimes, when there's a lot going on in life, and our days are pretty busy, the only time our mind has time to think is at night. This becomes a problem when we can't control how long we are thinking, what we are thinking about, and how to refocus our minds. This is where our next super-power, Super-Power #13, **The Journal in Your Mind**, comes in.

Are you ready to begin and help Shayna learn to fall asleep more easily? Touch your right knee with your left hand, and then your left knee with your right hand to show me that you're ready!

The Journal in Your Mind is a personal journal in your mind where you can write or sketch down any thoughts that are bothering you and that may be keeping you awake. I'd like you to create the journal now. What color is the cover of your journal? What color are the pages? What are you using to write or draw with—a pencil? A pen? Or are you using a crayon, marker, or colored pencil? Now, draw or write anything on your mind that may be bothering you and keeping you awake (or awake later). Close the cover of the journal when you're done—now those thoughts are gone and away, unless you open the journal and want to think about them another time.

Let's check in on Shayna. I hope that the strength of **The Journal in Your Mind** super-power helped her get to sleep!

Self-Control Academy strikes again! You guys are the best! Ok, draw a smiley face in the air, and let's see if all 13 coins come up.

Super-Power #14: Wrap Yourself in Blankets

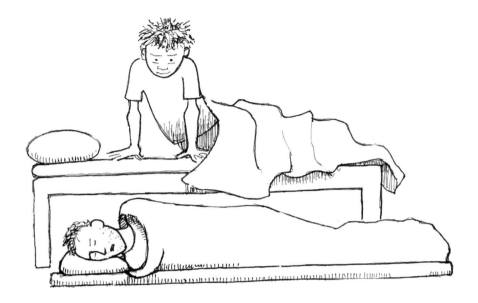

Flynn's body feels like it has to constantly move, even though he feels constantly tired. When evening approaches, it's like he has renewed energy from the school day, and does his homework upside down! Bedtime approaches. His feet are tapping; his arms are tapping with the effort of not jumping out of bed. Finally, at 11:00 p.m. he goes to his dad who is falling asleep on the couch. "Dad, I can't sleep!" "Yes you can, you just aren't trying enough. Go back to bed, I'll lay next to you on the floor." As soon as his dad's head hits the pillow, he's already snoring. "Why can't it be like that for me?" Flynn thinks grumpily.

Ok guys, we have to teach Flynn a way to make his body relax enough to get back to sleep. This is a way that I like to fall asleep myself, and it looks kind of like one of my favorite foods—a burrito!

Are you ready for Super-Power #14? Roll your neck in a circle one time if you are!

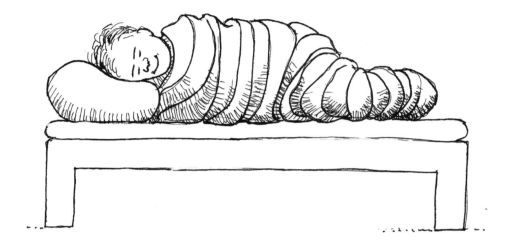

Here is how to do **Wrap Yourself in Blankets**. Snuggle up under the blanket—wrap it around either side of you tightly, like a burrito. Make sure that your head is sticking out of the blanket. If you would like, add another blanket on top. Do you like how it feels when you're wrapped up tightly? If you need help, ask a grown-up. Don't you feel calm and safe? Take a nice, deep breath. This will help you go to sleep.

Let's see how Flynn is doing. Do you think he was able to relax his body and fall asleep?

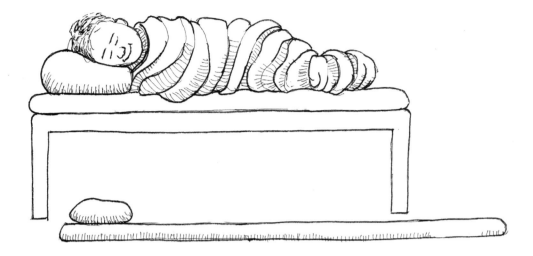

We are almost at graduation, and for good reason! Now, give yourselves a tight hug, and see if 14 coins appear.

Super-Power #15: Picture Your Calm and Happy Place

Max is afraid to sleep on his own. Every night, he wakes up, goes to his mom and dad's room, and asks them to sleep in his room. Everybody in the house is tired. When asked what he is afraid of, he says, "Everything." The room feels too dark, any noises feel too scary, shadows feel like monsters. One night, his mom and dad refuse to come and sleep in his room. He screams and cries. "I can't sleep without you! I can't, I can't, I can't!"

I think it's important to know that we can do things for ourselves and by ourselves. Over time, it will make you feel independent and, as a result, more confident and happy, trust me! Let's help Max learn how to sleep on his own. The first thing we need to teach him is to feel calm, and not afraid. That's where our last super-power, Super-Power #15, **Picture Your Calm and Happy Place**, comes in.

Close your eyes. What is one of the most happy, calm, and peaceful places that you can think of? Now think of what it looks like. Picture as many details as you can. Now, think of anything that you may feel in this special place. Picture as many details as you can. Now, think of anything you may hear in this special place. Picture as many details as you can. Now, think of anything you may smell in this special place. Picture as many details as you can. Where are you in this special place? What are you doing? Are you doing anything, or simply just being?

Let's see if the strength of the **Picture Your Calm and Happy Place** super-power helped Max fall asleep all on his own!

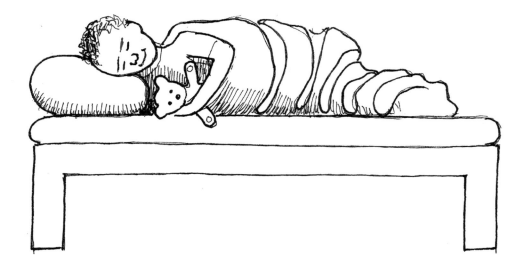

You did it! You helped Max, along with all of our friends, in such a kind and brave way. Take a deep breath in for three seconds, and breathe out for five seconds. Let's see if that breath blew the last coin onto the book, giving us all 15 coins!

Sum it Up

You saved the day! Doesn't it feel great?

You guys did it! You made it through Self-Control Academy, and did so stupendously! You helped kids learn how to manage some really tricky situations, which you think you may be going through as well (at least some of them), and I hope that you also learned how to manage the same tough stuff that crops up in everyday life.

See all the coins that you've earned? They just came to land on you as you're reading this, right this second. Where? I'm not sure. The coins go where they feel like they should go.

Nope, you can't see them, but I'm telling you they're there.

The coins that you've earned along this journey are here to assist you, and remind you that you're amazing, have awesome powers of self-control, and that they will help get you out of tough situations where you feel like your self-control may be too low.

Come back to this book if you need a reminder of that.

Now that you're certified Self-Control Super-Heroes, I expect you to wear this title with pride and honor. Be role models to your peers of what the meaning of self-control is.

Help others who don't have this super-power...yet. Teach them the ways of self-control learned in Self-Control Academy.

To sum it up

1. Even though we cannot change other people, or all situations that life throws our way, we are lucky enough to be gifted with the control to change our emotions and reactions to what life throws at us.

2. We are kind and helpful.

3. At the end of an argument, we make sure to end it with doing an act of kindness for the other person.

4. Being flexible is tough. When we say to friends that something is flexible, even when we don't always mean it, it helps us be the best friend that we can be.

5. Sleep is not over-rated. We all need it. Plus, there are ways we can make it easier to fall and stay asleep.

6. You CAN be in control. Believing that you have self-control is a lot of the battle.

7. Stop and think why you may have trouble focusing. It's ok if you don't understand something, and it shows that you're responsible for your learning when you ask for help.

8. Believe in the super-powers. Believe that they will make a difference in your life. Mostly, believe in yourself.

Until next time,

Self-Control

PART 2

FOR ADULTS

For Parents

Simple Adjustments to Your Existing Morning and Evening Routines to Make Those "Ahhh!" Moments Go More Smoothly!?

Hey, fellow parents!

I totally get how hectic life can be. I've been there and, honestly, I'm still there plenty. A big part of why I wanted to write this book was to pinpoint the most common parts of the day that I know feel most difficult for either myself or fellow parents, and offer simple-to-implement solutions.

This section is for you. It's simple, to the point, and offers some time-proven tips and tricks from my own household that have been shown to be very effective. To the point: my kids have gone to bed at 6:00 p.m. since they were eight months old. Please don't hate me. That's why I'm writing this book, now! You may already be doing some of these suggestions, so just gloss over the ones you're familiar with if necessary.

Morning routines

- If your child doesn't know how to read numbers, try and get them to recognize at least the number on the clock that represents wake-up time. There are clock solutions for falling/staying asleep that change color as well, but I always try to stay with the least amount of items that I have to purchase.

- My youngest child loves to sleep in, so she requires a few reminders a bit earlier than my older two, in addition to the strategies mentioned in the first part of the book. Instead of me having to do this (I am either getting dressed for work or, well, drinking my coffee and taking a minute for myself), I have my eldest daughter, who is an early riser, do the kind and gentle reminders. She needed some coaching initially in this regard. Guess what? Over time, my youngest child began waking up on her own when she was supposed to.

- I take out snacks/lunch the night before. The kids lay out their clothes for the next day, right down to gloves/coats/socks/shoes, so everything is set for a (mostly) smooth morning routine.

- We have designated morning coloring, playing, and reading time. If the kids can get dressed early enough, they have time to do a simple art project, read, or play. This usually acts as an incentive to get dressed quickly to have enough time for "Me Time," as we call it. We used to utilize a schedule, which looked something like the following (I actually had this on my fridge in the kitchen, and also in each child's room, until they were independent in this area). There is a downloadable version of the schedule at the end of the book, which can be downloaded at www.jkp.com/catalogue/book/9781785927591

Getting ready in the morning

1) Get out of bed ☐

2) Wash face ☐

3) Brush teeth ☐

4) Get dressed ☐

5) Do hair ☐

6) Eat breakfast ☐

7) Lunch in bag ☐

8) Check bag—"Do I have everything I need for school?" ☐

9) Coat and shoes on ☐

Getting ready in the morning: Visual schedule

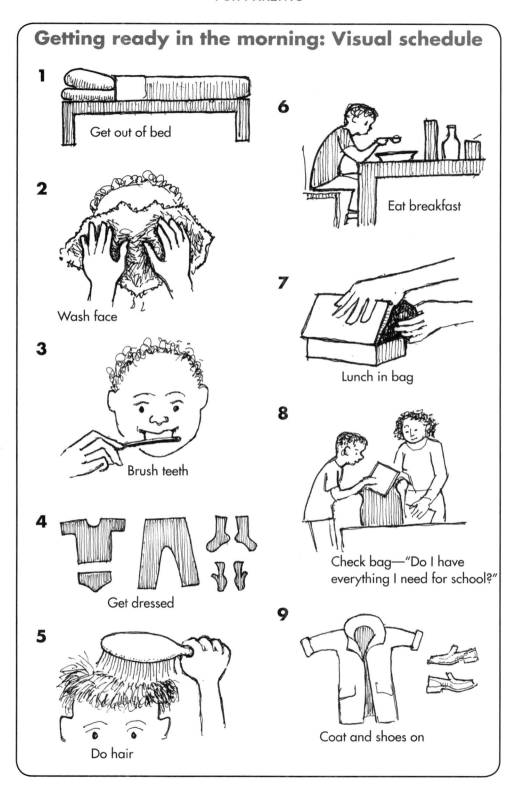

1 Get out of bed

2 Wash face

3 Brush teeth

4 Get dressed

5 Do hair

6 Eat breakfast

7 Lunch in bag

8 Check bag—"Do I have everything I need for school?"

9 Coat and shoes on

Homework routines

- We have a sensory toolbox, and each child gets what they need in order to focus best on their work. The most popular items lately have been noise-canceling headphones to block out noisy siblings (or music that I'm playing that is not always widely received), weighted items (yesterday, my youngest took out a weighted sock that I made because her math made her frustrated—her words, not mine), visual timers, and hand-made fidgets that I made with my kids.

- I play low-frequency classical music in the background (hence, the noise-canceling headphones for my eldest daughter, who doesn't like the music, but my younger two love it).

- My youngest child does her best focusing when standing.

- My middle child focuses best using an inclined surface and a tactile fidget; we use a binder tilted to the side.

- **Homework bins**: Each child has a shelf, with their name on it, in my den, with their own bin on it. In their bin, they keep important items that they don't want/don't need to bring back and forth, such as textbooks, homework passes, special pencils, password information for online homework accounts, etc. This set-up really helps keep them organized and independent in managing their own materials.

- We keep important and heavily used items for homework in a cup in the den and in the kitchen area too because our kids frequently do their homework there. Items include highlighters, pencils, erasers, scissors, glue sticks, etc.

- Our kids have a usual homework routine that they do, at this point, by rote. Even though they're different ages, it pretty much follows the same pattern. They start with the hardest subject, and work their way down to the easiest subject. The following is an example of a schedule that your kids can follow, where they check off as they go. (There is a downloadable version of the schedule at the end of the book, which can be downloaded at www.jkp.com/catalogue/book/9781785927591) You can modify this, accordingly. Try pairing each section with a visual timer, so that they can see how long they're expected to work at each section, and you may find that their attention and motivation will increase, especially for more difficult subjects. I usually allot one minute per year of age, before a two-minute break to get up and do a quick stretch before returning to work. This is an example for my eldest daughter. Yours may be different, based on age and area of most difficulty for your child(ren), but this formula works best for us.

Homework routine

1) Math—10 minutes ☐

2) Two-minute stretch ☐

3) Writing—10 minutes ☐

4) Two-minute stretch ☐

5) Spelling—10 minutes ☐

6) Two-minute break ☐

7) Dinner ☐

8) Reading—20+ minutes ☐

Homework routine: Visual schedule

Math symbols

Stretching

Spelling

Dinner

Reading

Helping siblings get along

- **Peace corner**: This is a designated area in our house where our kids know to go to work out arguments. This is the same area where we keep the box of sensory tools, so that they're accessible, if needed, by kids involved during this time. We have the steps in the work-it-out solution framed so that they follow this guide, especially when emotions are heated. We try to get involved in their arguments as little as possible, and stress the importance of them working out their issues independently. We explain that they have the tools to do so.

- We try to offer more than one area, when possible, for our kids to take space, when that is a choice they vocalize. I've noticed that the more they're provided with choice during these moments, the faster and easier they bounce back.

- We use the word "flexible" a lot in our daily conversations. We name it for them when we are flexible with them, and when we are flexible with each other. Having them begin interactions with a specific statement such as the one outlined in the first section ("Let's Take Turns Choosing What to Do") is especially helpful if you're finding that one child is having a hard day, or struggles with flexibility in general.

- When my kids were younger, we used color-coded visual sand timers that represented different time increments for sharing toys/games, when needed. They didn't need my help to use them, and using them alone felt, I think, "grown-up" and helped teach them autonomy when it came to social interaction and peer negotiation, as well as conflict resolution. We have three sand timers, for three, five, and seven minutes (they're green, black, and orange). Once in a while, the kids still pull the timers out if this issue crops up. They're used when one of my kids needs to cool off in a sensory area for a few minutes and wants a visual of how long he/she would like to stay there (at times they stay longer by choice); they also utilize them for completion of homework.

Evening routines

- My kids have a super-consistent schedule during the week. They know exactly what to expect the moment they get off the bus until the moment they go to sleep (during the week, because we are more flexible on the weekends). The times where it's different, I see a significant difference in my kids' sleep and consequent attention and behavior. I truly believe that knowing what to expect is calming, and sets the stage for a good night's sleep.

- Our evening routine consists of the following:
    1. coats/bags/shoes by the front door and on the hook
    2. have a bath
    3. pajamas
    4. homework—relaxing music playing in the background
    5. dinner
    6. reading
    7. bed.

- A schedule like the example below will allow your child/ren to take ownership of each part of the evening routine, while giving them control and understanding, and thus a sense of predictability and regulation. There is a downloadable version of the schedule, with two options, at the end of the book, which can be downloaded at www.jkp.com/catalogue/book/9781785927591.

- We talk and unwind during dinner. My kids wake up early and play in the mornings. This may not be for everyone, but it works for us. They go to bed at 6:00 p.m./6:30 p.m., and wake up at 6:00 a.m./6:15 a.m. No complaints!

- We don't do any overly active activities before bed. We don't do screen time at all during the week (but even on weekends, we don't watch in the evening or late afternoon hours). I would never tell you not to do those things, and I understand from personal experience that TV can be a lifesaver, I am just relaying my own experience with sleep and decreased screen time—during the week, at least. Some nights, I will do some yoga or a meditation story with my kids as a special activity if we have some extra time and they all finish their homework at a similar pace.

- When my kids were younger, I had our evening routine written down and scheduled to the minute! Well, looking back, that may have been a bit extreme, but I really think that having a set schedule and routine of everyone knowing exactly what to do, especially during weeknights, made the entire family (not just the kids) happier, and better rested for sure. The following is a sample schedule that we follow (we now know it automatically, but I had hand created it in the beginning, and laminated it lovingly, before thumbtacking it to my kitchen wall for anyone watching my children past 3:00 p.m. to follow to a T).

- Examples of calming activities before bed include coloring, building with manipulatives, reading, writing in a journal, etc.

Evening routines

1) Dinner ☐

2) Brush teeth ☐

3) Wash face ☐

4) Read for 20 minutes ☐

5) Bed ☐

I hope that some of these ideas were helpful to you, and can fit seamlessly into your existing routines!

XO,

Lauren

Evening routine: Visual schedule

Dinner

Brush teeth

Wash face

Reading

Bed

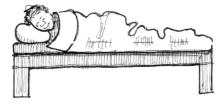

For Educators and Therapists

Tangibles and Supports for Kids to Make These Strategies More Concrete and Transfer into Everyday Life

Hey!

So, I've been in the school system for a long time, and have gone through a lot of high points in my career, and hit some more challenging situations. Teachers—I know how difficult it can be to implement strategies easily and successfully while managing large classes with kids of varying needs, and you're probably looking at this book and thinking, "Oh boy, another book. Ugh! I don't have the time." Therapists—I have been there. High mandates, high caseloads; who has the time to (a) read a book and (b) make cutesy little visuals that actually transfer those skills into the classroom?

Hence, I created this book. Probably the book I have been most excited to create. We don't have time to target every single skill for every part of the day. Just being real. So, my dear colleagues, I chose those times of the school day that are the hardest for our sweet kiddos, where we hear the most concerns that crop up, and areas where kids often struggle...recess/lunch, and friendships. We can also cover paying attention, since that gets brought up a ton, as well.

Let's simplify life. There are beautiful and ready-to-photocopy/laminate (you have a laminator, right?) desk strips, posters, and bracelets for kids at the end of the book (which can be downloaded at www.jkp.com/catalogue/book/9781785927591). However, I thought it might be nice to give some tangible ways to introduce each strategy presented in the three areas I just mentioned.

Before we begin, let's brainstorm some ways to maximize retention and transfer of strategies from these three areas into the kids' schema and toolbox of coping skills:

- **For the duration of approximately three months (taking into account holidays, school events, etc.), have your class/ children in your therapy group learn one new strategy each week.** This will total nine weeks. Introduce the strategy at the beginning of the week through reading the relevant chapter from the book. Follow this with a tangible activity described below. As the week progresses, add visuals (which can also be created by the children, and/or taken from this book) in frequented and appropriate areas throughout the classroom and school. Over the course of the week, continue to reinforce the strategy in one or more of the following ways:

  - **Have all the class/children in your therapy group draw a representation of each strategy as they're taught on different colored pieces of paper that can be hole-punched onto a keyring.** This is a tangible and child-created tool that can be taken anywhere with them and represents all of the strategies. It can be sent home, and all home-related strategies can be drawn/completed with caregivers and added to the keyring.

  - **Display a visual of the strategy being taught by the meeting area.** Remind the class/children in your therapy group at the beginning of the day of the strategy being reviewed.

  - **Embed wording consistent with the strategy, as appropriate, into classroom conversations and academic talk.**

  - **Write a reminder on the classroom board/therapy board during the morning meeting (or include this as a job for one of the children):** "Our strategy of the week is _____. What is one way that we may need to use it today to feel happy and have self-control? Can we think of a predictably difficult time of the day where using this strategy can help us?"

  - **Place the book, when not in use, in an area that is visually accessible to all the children.** Consider placing it in a book bin area with other calming books, or by itself in a cool-down area.

○ **Consider allowing different children to read specific sections aloud to the class.** This book focuses on building discussions, so why not have the children act as leaders in helping to foster and further develop the classroom/therapeutic community, while reinforcing that everyone has their "stuff" and it's ok to need a little help.

○ **Do you have a classroom newsletter?** If so, consider adding a small section where you talk about the "Strategy of the Week": name the strategy, ways kids are using it in the classroom, and how it is helpful.

○ **Consider lighting, music, and nutrition.** These are the building blocks, the base, that will affect your pupils' overall regulation. In the mornings, your pupils are more likely to be more tired, so consider utilizing brighter lighting (I recommend veering away from fluorescent), high-frequency music, and whole-class exercises with faster movements that cross the midline and have elements of vestibular input (where the head engages in rotational/up-and-down movement). In the afternoon (and particularly after recess/lunch/high-stimulation activities), consider dimming the lights (again, veering away from the use of fluorescents), utilizing low-frequency music, and engaging the class in exercises that are slower with elements of proprioception, mirroring (copying), and deep pressure.

Tangible activities for strategies
Thought Box

Materials: Empty tissue box, two sheets of different colored paper or index cards, paint/markers/stickers/art supplies of choice

A relatively simple way to make this idea tangible would be to give out two sheets of different colored paper (I have done this with green and red index cards—to minimize the cutting on my part—but if you would like the activity to be child driven, and to work on scissor skills, you can use construction paper). I like the red and green because, for many kids, green means go and red means stop.

Instruct the children that they're going to be decorating their Thought Boxes. Allow them to get as creative as they want. Remind them, as they go, of the purpose of the Thought Box. Have kids draw or write distracting thoughts on the red cards, and focused thoughts on the green cards. Ask them what color cards should go into the Thought Box (red). To make it fun, without it getting too silly, see if they can balance the most focused green card on their head (on their "brain") for ten seconds while standing perfectly still.

Squeeze Your Whole Body!

Materials: None

"Do you know how to make a muscle in your arm? Great, now relax the muscle." Most kids will probably say yes to the question—those who can't, model and assist. "Now, just like you made that muscle and then relaxed it, I want you to do the same for your whole body! Make a muscle in your whole body, hold it—1-2-3-4-5, and relax." Ask your pupils where they feel their wiggles. "Now, we're going to squeeze those wiggles out of our bodies when we make a muscle out of our whole body, ok? Ready—1-2-3-4-5, and relax. All the wiggles went away!"

Squeeze into a Ball

Materials: None

This is a great position that I have been cueing kids to utilize when sitting on the rug or at desks. It is grounding, as feet are planted on the floor and knees are pressing against the chest, while the child is actively hugging and squeezing themselves into a ball, providing deep pressure throughout the body. A good way to introduce this activity is to begin from a standing position—feet flat, a shoulder's width apart, arms hanging loosely at the sides, with eyes closed.

Say the following to the children: "You're a strong tree in a forest. Your feet are the roots of the tree that are weaving into the ground. Those roots are so strong; they don't bend in the wind. Your arms are branches that are firm against the wind. A gust blows by, but your strong roots keep you standing nice and tall. You're brave, strong, confident, and in control. When you're ready, open your eyes."

Now, transition them to sit. "Remember how you were so steady as a tree? It's the same thing during the Squeeze into a Ball exercise. Your feet stay planted, and you're steady, brave, strong, confident, and in control."

Take Space Inside Your Mind

Materials: Art supplies (this can be as simple or complex as you want to make it!)

Depending on how much time you can devote to this project (and how high a priority this particular strategy is for you), this activity can be as simple as a sketch or as complex as a 3D creation. Ask your class/children in your therapy group to think of a calm place they would like to take a break to, and think about when the outside world becomes too overwhelming. They can draw it simply with pencils, markers, or paint, or use playdough, cardboard, beads, or clay. The more control the child has over the activity, the more meaning it has, and the more willing they're likely to be to utilize the strategy.

Focus on One Detail

Materials: Cardboard paper towel rolls

This is a tangible way to show your pupils how to focus on one object in their visual environment. Tell them to close one eye, and look through the cardboard roll with the other eye. Ask them what they see in the environment that is most calming. You can also do this in the courtyard and lunch room to find focus points to use the next day.

Focus on Your Breathing

Materials: Pompoms, feathers, or another light object

It can be hard to visualize breathing. Have pupils break into pairs, with one laying down and one sitting up. The pupil laying down should place one pompom on their chest and one on their belly. Let the pupil sitting down know that they will be observing what happens to the pompoms. Using the format illustrated below, have them write or sketch their observations as the other breathes in, and as the other breathes out.

Breathe in—observations (chest)	Breathe in—observations (stomach)
Breathe out—observations (chest)	Breathe out—observations (stomach)

"Let's Take Turns Choosing What to Do"

Materials: Folders, paper, pencils

A nice idea to help children develop perspective for others and deepen friendships is to get to know friends and classmates in a structured and predictable way. This can be accomplished through the use of "Friendship Folders." Pair children up with either pre-written questions (and later, allow them to come up with their own, if able) or child-generated questions, and have them take turns asking questions about each other. Examples include: What's your favorite food? Do you have a pet? What's your favorite board game? Do you have siblings?

"Let's Take Space for Five Minutes"

Materials: Hula-hoops

Sometimes, it's important to show kids what personal space is, especially when they're in close quarters, arguments arise, and there is little room to take space from each other. This is a situation where they really need to take into account personal space. A good visual to show them how to do so is a picture of a "bubble of personal space." Break pupils into pairs. One child stands within the hula-hoop. The other child cannot enter that area.

Simple Steps to Solving Arguments

Materials: Visual of simple steps to solving arguments

Put the visual in an accessible area of your classroom or therapy area. Break pupils into groups of two. Provide them with a scenario where they have to act out an argument and then solve it using the steps in the visual. Video tape, and review as a class.

Provide miniature photocopies of the steps to solving arguments. Put on a keyring for each child. This is especially important for high-dysregulatory times of the day, such as recess and lunch.

Self-Control Gold Coin Reward Chart

This visual chart can be downloaded at www.jkp.com/catalogue/ book/9781785927591. It can be photocopied or laminated and placed at a child's desk, or at home on the fridge/table/wall, etc. As the child learns each strategy and implements it into his/her daily life, he/she can color in a coin on the chart. You may want to pair this with a small token reinforcement. After 5, the reinforcement may be a bit larger, and finally at 15, the child may choose a prize. This is particularly helpful in behavioral situations, where children are particularly motivated by token reinforcements, and even when they require a tangible reinforcement to color as they go to see their progress.

Directions: Color in each coin as the child earns it *throughout* the book. Allow a choice of coloring utensil to provide as much ownership over the process as possible.

Reminder Bracelets

The bracelets on the next pages will reinforce the 15 super-powers/ strategies that you have learned throughout this book. (You can download the bracelets from www.jkp.com/catalogue/book/9781785927591.) Children should wear them daily, depending on the area of concern that you wish to target. Please utilize fading prompts from adults, as this should, over time, allow these strategies to transform into habits naturally occurring across a range of environments. The bracelets are divided according to the five numbered chapters of this book.

Directions

1. Download and cut out the strips.

2. Photocopy them to use daily.

3. Or (the preferred option, if you have the means!) laminate a bracelet and circle the preferred super-power that you or the child chooses. This creates a durable bracelet for the child that he/she can use daily.

Getting ready in the morning

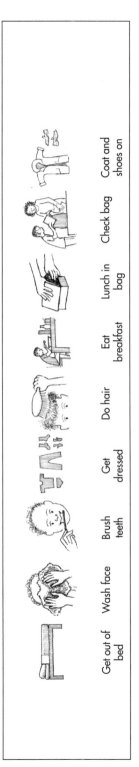

| Get out of bed | Wash face | Brush teeth | Get dressed | Do hair | Eat breakfast | Lunch in bag | Check bag | Coat and shoes on |

Paying attention

| Thought box | Squeeze your whole body | Squeeze into a ball |

Recess and lunch

| Take space in your mind | Focus on one detail | Focus on your breathing |

Friendship tips

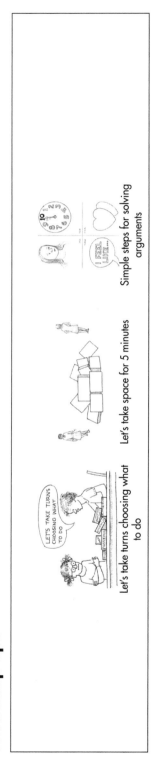

Let's take turns choosing what to do

Let's take space for 5 minutes

Simple steps for solving arguments

Bedtime

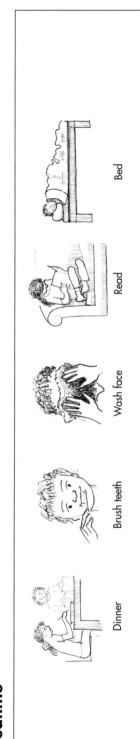

Dinner

Brush teeth

Wash face

Read

Bed

Morning Routines

Here is a sample schedule, with visuals, that your child/ren can check off as they go through each step. (You can download the schedule from www.jkp.com/catalogue/book/9781785927591.) This will allow them to take ownership of each part of the morning routine, while giving them control and understanding, and thus a sense of predictability and regulation (while getting everyone out on time!). Laminate or put into a pocket protector for increased durability.

Getting ready in the morning

1) Get out of bed ☐

2) Wash face ☐

3) Brush teeth ☐

4) Get dressed ☐

5) Do hair ☐

6) Eat breakfast ☐

7) Lunch in bag ☐

8) Check bag—"Do I have everything I need for school?" ☐

9) Coat and shoes on ☐

Getting ready in the morning: Visual schedule

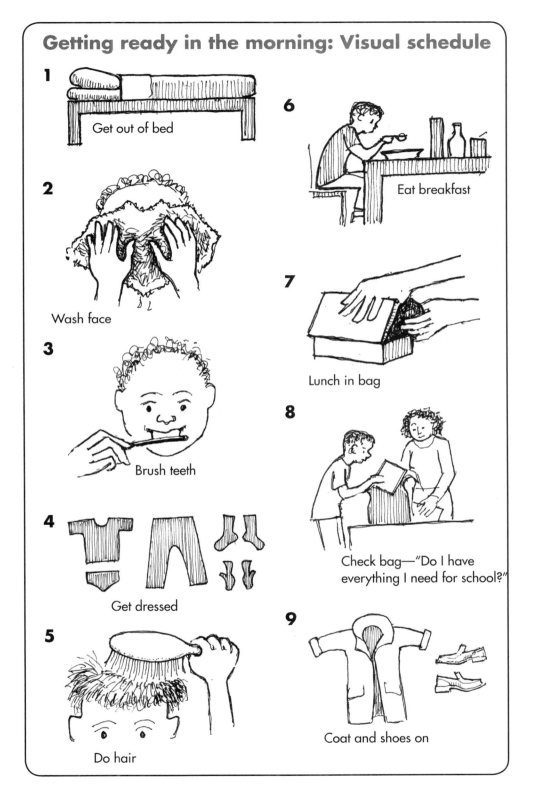

1 Get out of bed

2 Wash face

3 Brush teeth

4 Get dressed

5 Do hair

6 Eat breakfast

7 Lunch in bag

8 Check bag—"Do I have everything I need for school?"

9 Coat and shoes on

Homework Routines

Here is a sample schedule, with visuals, that your child/ren can check off as they go through each step. (You can download the schedule from www.jkp.com/catalogue/book/9781785927591.) This will allow them to take ownership of each part of the homework process, while giving them control and understanding, and thus a sense of predictability and regulation. Pairing this schedule with a visual timer allows for kids to know how long they're expected to focus on a particular task before engaging in a short break, if needed, which maximizes motivation and attention to task. Laminate or put into a pocket protector for increased durability.

Homework routine

1) Math—10 minutes ☐

2) Two-minute stretch ☐

3) Writing—10 minutes ☐

4) Two-minute stretch ☐

5) Spelling—10 minutes ☐

6) Two-minute break ☐

7) Dinner ☐

8) Reading—20+ minutes ☐

Homework routine: Visual schedule

Math symbols

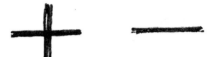

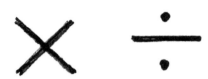

Stretching

Spelling

Dinner

Reading

Evening Routines

Here is a sample schedule, with visuals, that your child/ren can check off as they go through each step. (You can download the schedule from www.jkp.com/catalogue/book/9781785927591.) This will allow them to take ownership of each part of the evening routine, while giving them control and understanding, and thus a sense of predictability and regulation. Laminate or put into a pocket protector for increased durability. There are two options below. One has a token reinforcement built in, with seven boxes to be checked off for every night that your child sleeps through the night independently and without waking up (or to your own specifications). At the end of the seven days, your child can get a prize that you decide on together— but remember, the element of choice really affects overall behavior and self-regulation, so the more control over the process you provide (while, of course, setting boundaries), the more success you're likely to have!

Evening routine 1

1) Dinner ☐

2) Brush teeth ☐

3) Wash face ☐

4) Read for 20 minutes ☐

5) Bed ☐

6) I slept the whole night! ☐

7) 1-2-3-4-5-6-7 = Prize! ☐

Dinner

Brush teeth

Wash face

Reading

Bed

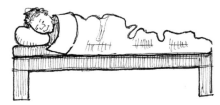

1-2-3-4-5-6-7 = Prize!

I slept the whole night

Evening routine 2

1) Dinner ☐

2) Brush teeth ☐

3) Wash face ☐

4) Read for 20 minutes ☐

5) Bed ☐

6) I slept the whole night! ☐

Dinner

Brush teeth

Wash face

Reading

Bed

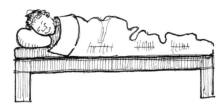

I slept the whole night

Desk Strip/Table Strip Reminders

These strips can be downloaded from www.jkp.com/catalogue/ book/9781785927591. They can be photocopied or laminated, and placed on the floor, at a desk/table, or on the wall, as a visual reminder of the 15 super-power strategies learned in this book. Since some of these strategies are more geared towards home use (i.e. waking up, going to bed), and others are aimed more at school function (such as recess/lunch), not all 15 need to be in the same area.

Getting ready in the morning

| Get out of bed | Wash face | Brush teeth | Get dressed | Do hair | Eat breakfast | Lunch in bag | Check bag—"Do I have everything I need for school?" | Coat and shoes on |

Paying attention

Thought box

Squeeze your whole body

Squeeze into a ball

Recess and lunch

Take space in your mind

Focus on one detail

Focus on your breathing

Friendship tips

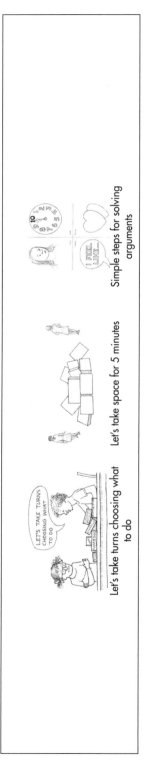

Let's take turns choosing what to do

Let's take space for 5 minutes

Simple steps for solving arguments

Bedtime

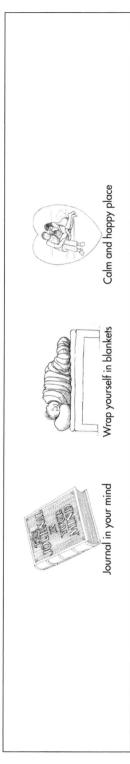

Journal in your mind

Wrap yourself in blankets

Calm and happy place

Self-Control Certificate
for 1 Super-Power

This is the certificate for when the child has mastered one super-power. (The template can be downloaded from www.jkp.com/catalogue/book/9781785927591.) Fill in the specific super-power on the line above the image.

CONGRATULATIONS!

You have mastered
the super-power of

_____

Date: _____

Adult signature: _____

Signature of Self-Control: *Self-Control*

Self-Control Diploma
for All 15 Super-Powers

This is the diploma for when the child has mastered all 15 super-powers. (It can be downloaded from www.jkp.com/catalogue/book/9781785927591.)

CONGRATULATIONS

on graduating from Self-Control Academy!

You are now an official Self-Control Super-Hero!

Date: _____

Adult signature: _____

Signature of Self-Control: *Self-Control*